Heidegger and Christianity

John Macquarrie

Heidegger and Christianity

The Hensley Henson Lectures 1993–94

Continuum · New York

1999

The Continuum Publishing Company
370 Lexington Avenue, New York, NY 10017

Library of Congress Cataloging-in-Publication Data

Macquarrie, John.
 Heidegger and Christianity : Hensley Henson
lectures, 1993–1994 / John Macquarrie.
  p. cm.
 Includes bibliographical references and index.
 ISBN 0-8264-1171-1
 1. Heidegger, Martin, 1889–1976. 2. Heidegger,
Martin, 1889–1976—Influence. 3. Theology,
Doctrinal—History—20th century. 4. Philosophy
and religion—History—20th century. I. Title.
B3279.H79M257 1994
193—dc20
            94–20201
            CIP

Printed in the United States of America

Contents

Preface

I wish to thank the Board of the Faculty of Theology at the University of Oxford for honouring me with an invitation to give the Hensley Henson Lectures for 1993–4. In the letter of invitation, it was stated that, according to the terms of Bishop Henson's Bequest, the subject of the lectures should be 'the appeal to history as an integral part of Christian apologetics', but the letter went on to say, 'it should be stressed that this subject may be taken in a very wide sense'. I intend to avail myself of the latitude which these words allow. I shall not consider any particular historical event or series of events in their bearing on Christianity, but raise the more general question of the status of time and history in relation to Christian thought.

Christianity and many other religions have had a somewhat ambiguous relation to time and history. On the one hand, history has been seen as a vehicle for God's self-communication to the human race. On the other hand, God and all that is most real is supposed to be beyond history, and untouched by the passage of time.

There is little doubt that at the present time the temporal and the historical have acquired a new importance in human thinking. There is a tendency to see everything as swept along in the flux of becoming. Nothing remains static. Even theologians have come to doubt whether such notions as 'immutability' and 'impassibility' are essential characteristics of God, though they were for long considered to be such. Thus we find the theologian Friedrich Gogarten asserting that whereas in earlier centuries, the events of history were supposed to take place on, so to speak, a permanent stage provided by metaphysics, that situation has now been reversed. The permanent framework has disappeared, and metaphysical systems are themselves regarded as products of history, rising and eventually decaying with changing situations. This might be called 'secularity' in the strict sense of the word – everything is embraced and given its character by the *saeculum* or age, so that secularization is simply historicization.

Is everything then plunged into a thorough relativism or even that nihilism which Nietzsche foresaw? One way of exploring such questions will be to take the work of a twentieth-century philosopher, Martin Heidegger, who gave a central place in his thinking to the temporality and historicality not only of human existence but of being generally. By attending to his concepts of time and history and also to his views on religion and theology, we may learn something of the impact on Christianity of the contemporary concern with time.

Oxford, 1 January 1994   John Macquarrie

Career and Early Writings

The significance of time and history for human life and indeed for all reality has been recognized from the earliest times. On the whole, the religions have tended to look beyond the transient events which we perceive going on within us and around us, and have sought a reality that stands above the flux and remains immune to change and decay. A contrast was made between the fleeting life of the creature and the enduring reality of God. So we read in the Hebrew scriptures:

> All flesh is grass,
>   and all its beauty is like the flower of the field.
> The grass withers, the flower fades;
>   but the word of our God will stand for ever. (Isa. 40. 6, 8)

This is not a denial of the reality of what goes on in this world – indeed, the biblical writers believed that God is keenly interested in the created order, and that he makes history itself a vehicle for his self-revelation to the human race. There is no acosmism in Jewish or Christian teaching, that is to say, no attempt to claim that the events of time are somehow illusory, as some of the religions of the further east come near to doing. Yet the 'really real', the ground on which everything rests, is above or beyond time. It is true that in the Hebrew scriptures God is sometimes depicted in anthropomorphic terms. He forms plans and then carries them out, such as the creation of the world; he is subject to changing moods, such as anger; he may even on occasion repent of what he has done. But the temporal order is a secondary reality and behind or beyond it is the eternal God. So Paul in the early years of Christianity declares: 'We look not to the things that are

seen but to the things that are unseen; for the things that are seen
are transient (*proskaira*), but the things that are unseen are
eternal (*aionia*)' (II Cor. 4, 18). Of course, as both Jewish and
Christian thought became increasingly affected by Greek influences, the supratemporal nature of God was emphasized, and
adjectives such as 'immutable' and 'impassible' became virtually
defining characteristics of deity.

In the earliest days of Greek philosophy, there was a different
form of this tension between the temporal and the eternal, the
historical and the suprahistorical. It is personified in the contrast
(or alleged contrast) between Heraclitus and Parmenides, both of
whom flourished in the sixth century before Christ. Heraclitus
compared the world to a great fire in which everything is involved
constantly in change. He is said to have taught that 'all things are
in process (*panta chorei*)' and, comparing the things of the world
to the flow of a river, declared that you can never step into the
same river twice.[1] But Heraclitus was not teaching that there is
just a meaningless jumble of events. There is a principle of order
and coherence among them called the Logos, which relates even
opposites and maintains a unity in the midst of the strife.
Heraclitus can also speak of God. This is not a creator God and it
is hard to know whether he is distinct from the world itself, but,
anticipating Nicholas of Cusa by two thousand years, Heraclitus
represents this God as a 'coincidence of opposites,' saying 'God is
day night, winter summer, war peace, satiety hunger, all the
opposites'[2] and presumably this God is the Logos under another
name. So although Heraclitus differed from the biblical writers in
apparently moving the weight of reality from the eternal to the
temporal, the result was not nihilism and the divine did not
disappear. There is a charming story about Heraclitus which tells
that one day in cold weather he was trying to keep warm beside a
stove in the rather humble cottage in which he lived. Some
strangers arrived and were surprised to find the eminent
philosopher in such straitened circumstances. But he encouraged
them to come in, telling them 'even the gods present themselves
here'.[3] Perhaps Justin the Martyr knew this story, and he includes
Heraclitus along with Socrates when he speaks of those Greeks
who had lived by the Logos even before the time of Christ, for

there is some analogy between the story and the Christian doctrine of an incarnation of the Logos in history. But the point of including it here is to show that a philosophy which gives the primacy in its thinking to change and process is not necessarily atheistic.

The great contemporary of Heraclitus was Parmenides, and he is generally supposed to have taken an opposite position to that of Heraclitus. His philosophy has been summarized as follows: '[The world] is like a sphere, single, indivisible and homogeneous, timeless, changeless and, since motion is itself one form of change, motionless as well. It has in fact no perceptible qualities whatever.'⁴ The events which we perceive by the senses are only the surface play, as it were. The reality behind is immutable. If one took this view in its extreme form, it would be just as inherently implausible as the view that everything is in flux with no permanency of structure or order. Furthermore, I think both views in their extreme forms would be incompatible with Christianity.

But just as we saw that Heraclitus modifies his teaching that everything is in process to allow for the unifying or gathering activity of the Logos, so Parmenides finds it impossible to deny that the world which every day confronts our eyes possesses some reality. It is, he thinks, a world of seeming or appearance contrasted with a world of being, but appearance contains elements of truth, even if they are mingled with falsehood. Probably the most famous aphorism of Parmenides was his saying that 'being and thinking are the same' (*to gar auto noein estin te kai einai*).⁵ The translation given here has been contested on the grounds that it gives too subjective a flavour to Parmenides and reads into him in an anachronistic manner the philosophy of German idealism. Other translations are possible, but I shall mention only one, the one adopted by Heidegger: 'Being and the thinking of being are the same.' This asserts an intimate and fundamental relation between being and the human thinker, the only being (at any rate, on this planet) who thinks of being and seeks an understanding of being.

This mention of Heidegger brings us to our main theme after our brief detour through the pre-Socratic philosophers. But that detour has served a purpose, for it has brought clearly before us some important characteristics of Heidegger's philosophy, characteristics which belonged to it from beginning to end. The first point is his constant striving to overcome the dichotomies that have been so typical of Western thinking and to show that they grew out of what was originally a unity. The tendency in this case is exemplified by Heidegger's treatment of Heraclitus and Parmenides. They are not so much opposite to one another as complementary. Other dualisms are likewise broken down, for instance, realism and idealism, perception and understanding, nature and history. The second point is the assertion of the essential link between man and being. Heidegger in fact rarely uses words such as 'man' or 'woman' or the adjective 'human'. He prefers to speak of *Dasein*, a German word meaning 'being there' and generally left untranslated in English versions of Heidegger. It stresses the connection with being (*Sein*). *Dasein* is not synonymous with 'human being' but is, in Heidegger's words, 'a pure expression of being'.[6] He also calls it a 'clearing',[7] like a clearing in a forest, the place or the 'there' where being is brought to light. The third point is that the discussion of Heraclitus and Parmenides draws our attention to Heidegger's high estimate of the early Greek thinkers. They were the first to ask the question of being and the originators of the history of Western thought. In Heidegger's view, the question of being was soon lost from sight and the beings, the things which make up the world, became the primary concern for human investigation. This 'forgetting of being', as he calls it, has been endemic in the West, and has reached its climax in the technological age. We have become 'rich in things and poor in soul'. Our very status as *Dasein* is threatened as human beings themselves are subordinated into what they have themselves created, the machinery of production and consumption. But before we consider the details of Heidegger's thinking, it will be useful to trace the outlines of his career and see some of the influences which shaped his thought and some of the stages through which it passed.

Martin Heidegger was born in 1889 in the small country town of Messkirch. This town is situated in the state of Baden, which occupies the extreme south-western corner of Germany, stretching along the eastern bank of the Rhine. Baden contains the mountainous region called the Black Forest, with peaks rising to between four thousand and five thousand feet. Much of the land is covered by woodland and farms. The people are mainly Catholic and conservative. The principal city is Freiburg im Bresgau, the seat of a university and of a Catholic archbishop.

Martin's father, Friedrich Heidegger, was head sexton of St Martin's Church in Messkirch. Friedrich had a special care for the clocktower and bells of the church, and this must have impressed his son, for many years later Heidegger tells how the ringing of these bells was associated in his mind with time and temporality.[8]

Growing up within sight and sound of the parish church, the young Martin was a keen Catholic and almost inevitably he seemed destined for the priesthood. For some years he attended a Jesuit seminary and later felt able to write: 'Without my theological origin, I would never have attained to the way of thinking.'[9] Especially he was beginning to see the importance of interpretation and hermeneutics. He was clearly a student of very high intelligence, and the clergy took an interest in forwarding his career. An event which was to prove much more important than it seemed on the surface took place in 1907, when Heidegger was eighteen. One of the priests, Fr Conrad Gröber (of whom we shall hear more later) presented the young man with a book. It was by the famous philosopher Franz Brentano, still alive at that time, and it dealt with the several different meanings of 'being' in the works of Aristotle. Not all eighteen-year-olds would appreciate such a present, but this book awakened in Heidegger the philosophical quest which kept him occupied for the rest of his life – the quest for the meaning of being.

In 1910 Heidegger went on to the University of Freiburg. He enrolled in theology but found he had still time to read philosophy. He had already discovered the works of Edmund Husserl, and tells us that he kept both volumes of his *Logical Investigations* in his desk.[10] The pull of philosophy was strong, and after two years Heidegger gave up his theological studies and thereafter devoted himself to philosophy. Husserl himself became professor of philosophy at Freiburg in 1916 and Heidegger enthusiastically adopted the phenomenological approach to philosophical problems. To quote his own words about this early period of his life: 'Thus was I brought to the path of the question of being, illumined by the phenomenological method, now stirred in a different way than had happened on reading Brentano's book. But the path of questioning became longer than I suspected. It demanded many stops, detours and wrong paths.'[11]

Heidegger's move from theology to philosophy does raise questions about his significance for theology. Actually he continued to attend some theological lectures, but his attitude toward theology became increasingly ambiguous as the years passed. By the end of 1918, by which time he had married a Lutheran bride, Elvire Petri, Heidegger had ceased to be a practising Catholic, though he claimed that he never left the Catholic Church. After his appointment to the chair of philosophy at Marburg in 1923, Heidegger engaged in active dialogue with Protestant theologians there, including Rudolf Bultmann, Paul Tillich and Rudolf Otto. Despite his equivocal remarks about Christian theology and the belief of some critics that he was an atheist, it may be affirmed that no philosopher had more influence than Heidegger on the theology of the twentieth century. For proof of this, we have only to look at the testimonies of some leading theologians. Bultmann and Tillich have been open in acknowledging their debt. Among Catholics, Karl Rahner said that he had many professors, but one teacher, Heidegger.[12] The opinions expressed by philosophers have been both more varied and more cautious. Hans-Georg Gadamer, in a memorial address, was very positive: 'It was Christianity that provoked and kept alive [Heidegger's] thought; it was the ancient transcendence and not modern secularity that spoke through him.'[13] But another former student of Heidegger's, Karl Löwith, has written that Heidegger's philosophy 'is in its very essence a theology without God'.[14] I suspect that the expression, 'a theology without God' is self-contradictory, but that would depend on the question of just how one understands the word 'God' and we shall see that Heidegger – perhaps quite properly – leaves this word shrouded in some obscurity.

It was, perhaps, during his years at Marburg that Heidegger was at his most creative. For several years he published virtually nothing, but he was working out his ideas at that time. We now have access to them, for in 1975, about a year before his death, there was begun the publication of his complete works, expected to run to about one hundred volumes and including not only writings thitherto published but also his lecture courses, reconstructed from his own notes and the notes taken by students. The course for 1925 was entitled *History of the Concept of Time*, and fills a substantial volume of more than three hundred pages. The work is important for at least two reasons. The first is that it is a significant step towards Heidegger's *magnum opus*, *Being and Time*, which followed it two years later. The second reason is that the course of lectures shows the centrality of the problem of time in Heidegger's philosophy.

A question which is not clearly answered in these 1925 lectures and which will come up again concerns the nature of phenomenology. Husserl believed that phenomenology is purely descriptive of that which is presented in and to consciousness, and therefore that it should 'bracket' or lay aside questions about the existence, origin, causation and so on of what is thus presented. Heidegger sometimes speaks in this way too, for instance, he says that phenomenology is 'a pure methodological concept which only specifies the *how of the research*'.[15] He holds therefore that such research must be, in a methodological sense, atheistic, in the same sense that the natural sciences are atheistic, that is to say, they do not bring in God as an 'explanation' for anything. Later on, however, he tells us that phenomenological research is 'the investigation of entities with regard to their being'.[16] But must not such an investigation come eventually to the problem of theism versus atheism? We must not lose sight of this apparent inconsistency in Heidegger's appeal to phenomenology.

Unfortunately, the course of lectures on the concept of time came to a halt with the end of the semester, before Heidegger got to the concluding section, which had been advertised as 'The Exposition of Time Itself' but had not been written. One cannot help wondering if professors sometimes arrange their lectures in such a way that the end of term will come before the most difficult questions have to be faced.

Heidegger's major work, *Being and Time* (*Sein und Zeit*) appeared in 1927. It was immediately recognized as a highly important contribution to philosophy. Looking back thirty years after its publication, Richard Kroner, who had been a colleague of Heidegger in the philosophy department at Freiburg, wrote: 'If one considers that in the academic world of that period philosophy was almost exclusively taught in lectures on epistemology, logic, ethics or aesthetics, it is astounding how boldly and self-assuredly Heidegger declared that such a division into various disciplines could not do justice to the most essential and authentic problem of philosophy. This problem, he insisted, is Being, undivided and all-embracing. I admit that I read his work with a breathless tension. I also used it in my seminars at the University of Kiel. Although I never became a Heideggerian, I could not escape being attracted by the unusual force of his thinking and way of speaking.'[17]

Being and Time, however, was a much misunderstood book. Perhaps the reason is that like the lectures of 1925, it remained unfinished. The early editions of the book carried on the title page the words 'First Half'. The second half was to have been a 'destructuring' or 'dismantling' (*Destruktion*) of the history of philosophy in confirmation of the argument of the first half. But even the first half was incomplete, and again we are out of luck. The text as Heidegger left it ends with a question: 'Does time itself manifest itself as the horizon of Being?'[18] – the very question to which this course of lectures is seeking an answer.

From the seventh edition of 1935 onward, the words 'First Half' were omitted. Of course, one may say that the book was completed in the many works which its author produced after 1927, though not in accordance with his original plan. The path he had meant to follow had broken off. We remember that Heidegger's lifelong aim was to struggle with the question of meaning of Being, that is to say, Being in the widest sense, Being as such, *das Sein überhaupt*. As we shall see, he believed that the way into that question is to question the being of the questioner. We recall that he had already come to the view that *Sein* and *Dasein* are intimately related. The analysis of *Dasein*'s existence in *Being and Time* was meant to be only the foundation (*Fundamentalontologie*) for the main investigation into the meaning of Being as such. So the book was misunderstood if taken primarily as a book about the existence of man, a kind of manifesto of existentialism. This impression was reinforced by Sartre's popularization of some of Heidegger's ideas in his book, *Being and Nothingness*. According to Sartre, existentialism is a humanism, indeed, in the book just mentioned, it comes close to being a nihilism, with man the measure of all things. Heidegger's views were very different, though sometimes he does seem to speak with a voice very much like Sartre's. So if he was misunderstood, it was largely his own fault.

Several important works, most of them fairly brief, appeared in the years following the publication of *Being and Time*. These included: (1) *What Is Metaphysics?* – his inaugural lecture when he returned to the University of Freiburg as Husserl's successor in the chair of philosophy in 1928; the lecture was published in 1929 and later a postscript was added, and later still an introduction. (2) *Kant and the Problem of Metaphysics*, a discussion of Kant's treatment of time in the two editions of the first *Critique*, also published in 1929. (3) *Introduction to Metaphysics*, which was based on lectures given in 1935, and may be regarded as a sequel to the inaugural lecture. (4) *On the Essence of Truth*, an important essay enlarging on the concept of truth taught in *Being and Time*. (5) Several essays on poetry, especially that of Friedrich Hölderlin. (6) An important piece on art, *The Origin of the Work of Art*, 1935.

But it was during this time that history broke rudely into the apparently uneventful life of Heidegger, as also into the lives of millions of other Germans, and before long into the lives of people all over the world. After the harsh treaty ending the Great War, Germany was in a very poor state, with the economy depressed, high inflation, and mass unemployment. The government seemed unable to improve the situation and there was widespread fear that the Communists might take over. It was a fertile situation for any demagogue who could capture the ear of the people. Such a one was Adolf Hitler, who played on the miseries and fears of the people and gained a large and increasing following. Among those who fell under the spell of National Socialism was Martin Heidegger. To this day there is controversy over the depth of his involvement with the Nazis, and the extent to which this involvement had its roots in his philosophy. *The Encyclopedia Britannica* passes over the relationship as a 'flirtation' but in the case of a serious-minded man like Heidegger, there was surely more to it than that. At the opposite extreme there are some, including the respected academic Hans Jonas, who have condemned Heidegger very severely and believe that his entire philosophy has been discredited by his action at that time.

I do not wish to interrupt the argument of this exposition on Heidegger and theology by being drawn into a long and, in all probability, inconclusive political discussion of events in the inter-war years. The matter is too important to be ignored and will be treated in chapter 8. For the moment I content myself with stating the bare facts. Hitler came to power quite constitutionally in January, 1933. In April of the same year, Heidegger was unanimously elected by his academic colleagues to be Rector of Freiburg University. In May he joined the National Socialist Party, though presumably he was already a supporter. Next year, 1934, he resigned the Rectorship. From then on, he distanced himself from the Party, but when the German universities were purged or 'de-nazified' after the war, he was forbidden to teach because of his earlier involvement. But as this was not considered very serious, the ban was lifted in 1950 and Heidegger went on teaching and writing until his retirement in 1959. One of those who supported his restitution was the cleric Conrad Gröber who had once given him the book by Brentano and was now Archbishop of Freiburg.

During the period when he was forbidden to teach and then after his restoration Heidegger produced several significant works. (1) Very important was the *Letter on Humanism*, addressed originally to the French philosopher Jean Beaufret, but intended for a wider public. In this letter, Heidegger makes clear the differences between himself and Sartre, and in particular that he does not think of the human mind as the subjective source for our understanding of Being. Rather, the *Dasein* is the recipient of Being's 'address' and Heidegger reinterprets *Being and Time* in a manner which leads away from the anthropocentrism characteristic of Sartre at that time. (2) The nature of thinking and the closely related subject of language were examined in such important works as *Was heisst Denken?* (1954), *Gelassenheit* (1957) and *Unterwegs zur Sprache* (1959), all of them translated into English, though the titles of the translations are not always clearly related to the original German titles. (See bibliography for details.) (3) Questions of religion and theology are mostly to be found in various collections of essays from this period: *Identität und Differenz* (1957) treats of onto-theology, the ontological difference and the overcoming of metaphysics. *Zeit und Sein* (1962) obviously reverses the title of Heidegger's major work published thirty-five years earlier, and was originally to have been the title for a division of that work, though this division was never written. This late writing cannot be considered as the fulfilling of Heidegger's intention of 1927, but it could be regarded as a kind of coping-stone to his philosophical work as a whole. (4) Heidegger's long-standing interest in the history of philosophy from early Greek thought onwards continued in these later years, the most obvious achievement being his lengthy work on Nietzsche (1961). These later writings will all engage our attention as we go along.

It is already clear from our sketch of Heidegger's career, so far as we have followed it, that he was a thinker who never decided that he had got to the end. So far as he found an answer to any question, that led to a new one. The path always continued.

Some students of Heidegger's work have seen in it two distinct stages or periods, and talk about the early Heidegger and the later Heidegger, or even about Heidegger I and Heidegger II, almost as if they were different persons. Obviously there are quite important differences between what we find in his early thinking, as expressed most comprehensively in *Being and Time*, and what we find him saying at later stages in his career. Heidegger himself tended to play down the attempt to contrast his earlier and later thought. He did acknowledge, as we have noted, that the path on which he originally set out had broken off. He would not have denied that there had been a turn (*Kehre*) in the road which he was following. But he was unhappy with suggestions that this amounted to a reversal. His aim from the first had been to rekindle interest in the question about the meaning of Being as such. Those who talked most of a reversal were those who had fallen into the Sartrean error of supposing that *Being and Time* is primarily a philosophical anthropology – though I did point out that Heidegger himself could not be altogether exculpated if people did make this mistake.

Nevertheless, when we look at Heidegger's work as a whole, we do notice some quite major shifts. Perhaps the most obvious is that there is a shift of focus from the *Dasein* known in human existence to Being in the most universal sense. A second point is that the scientific (*wissenschaftlich*) character of the phenomenological method used in the analysis of *Dasein* gives way to an appreciation of the language of the poet in interpreting the meaning of Being and *Dasein*'s relation to Being. There is a change too in the character of the thinking. In the early work, the thinking of the philosopher is investigative and active. In the later work, thinking becomes meditative, even passive, so that some critics have claimed to see mystical tendencies in Heidegger. Very important too is the change in the concept of the world. In the early thinking, the world is an instrumental system, and things lie ready-to-hand for the use of the *Dasein* in everyday concerns. But in the later writings, the world is no longer primarily a workshop but has a dignity in its own right, so to speak. Things are not just 'equipment' (*Zeug*) but are constituted by the 'fourfold' of heaven and earth, gods and mortals. This is also a good illustration of how the language of poetry, even a quasi-mythological language, has replaced phenomenological analysis.

These changes in Heidegger, though they do not constitute a 'reversal,' are sufficiently substantial to show a definite 'turn'. Perhaps it could be summarized under the last of the points which I noted, 'from phenomenology to thought', and this phrase was in fact chosen by William Richardson as the subtitle of his magisterial exposition of Heidegger's philosophy.

As we shall see, the turn or change began very soon after the writing of *Being and Time*, when Heidegger realized that he would have to look for a different path from the one he was planning to follow. But the turn was not an abrupt one, and we can observe it going on over several years.

Perhaps, as John Caputo has suggested, we should think not just of one turn in Heidegger's thought but of several turns.[19] He mentions as the first the turn away from Catholicism to a kind of independent Protestantism in Heidegger's early years of teaching at Marburg. Then there was the turn to something close to atheism or even nihilism extending perhaps through the time of his involvement with National Socialism. But already during these years there are hints of a 'return' – not indeed to his original Catholicism, but to what Richard Kroner called 'Heidegger's private religion'[20] which was perhaps as much derived from Greek sources as from biblical ones.

In 1949 Heidegger wrote a short piece which is quite different from most of his writings. It was called *Der Feldweg*, or in English *The Country Path*, and describes a path leading through the countryside near to Heidegger's home town of Messkirch. This writing, I say, is different from most of Heidegger's work. It is not overtly philosophical, but one does not need much imagination to see this path as an allegory of Heidegger's own path of thinking, though whether he intended it to be taken that way, I would not claim to know. The path leaves the town and proceeds through the fields in the direction of some woods. Near the edge of the woods stood a tall oak, with a wooden bench beneath it. Heidegger remembers how in his youth he used to sit on that bench studying the great masters of thought and trying to understand what they were saying. At that time in his life, I suppose Aristotle must have been one of the authors on whom he lavished special attention, perhaps also Heraclitus and Parmenides, certainly St Thomas and the scholastics, possibly even Nietzsche and Husserl. The path skirted the woods, where the men of the neighbourhood, including Heidegger's father, had each his own woodpile where he would gather fallen boughs. And here Heidegger thinks of the oak as symbolizing that fourfold nature which is in all things, though he does not explicitly mention it as a philosophical doctrine. What he says is this: 'The hardness and smell of the oakwood began to speak clearly of the slow and lasting way in which the tree grew. The oak itself proclaimed that all that lasts and bears fruit is founded on such growth alone; that growth means to lie open to the span of the heavens and, at the same time, to have roots in the dark earth; that everything real and true only prospers if mankind fulfills at the same time the two conditions of being ready for the demands of highest heaven and of being safe in the shelter of the fruitful earth. The oak continually repeats this to the country lane, whose track runs past it ... The kingdom of all living things which grow around the country lane offers a whole world in microcosm. The very ineffability of their language proclaims, as Meister Eckhart, that old master of life, says, God, first God.'

These sentences from the essay show us how Heidegger's philosophy, in spite of its complexities and sophistication, has its origins in very simple experience. But we have to be ready to hear such things. Contemporary man, Heidegger believes, does not hear the message. 'Man seeks in vain to reduce the world to his plans if he is not attuned to the message of the country lane.'

The lane ends in some marshes by the riverside. Turning round, we see it leading back toward the town. We can also see the tower of St Martin's church, and as we climb towards the town, we hear the bell ringing the hour, that bell which Heidegger's father had tended and which had first made him think of time and temporality. After the bell, there is silence. To quote the essay again, 'The eternal sameness of things surprises and sets free. The message of the country lane is now quite clear. Is it the soul, or the world, or God who is speaking?'[21]

Is it the soul or the world or God who is speaking? Heidegger does not answer his own question. Perhaps he would have said that it is the voice of Being, which we human beings may name as the soul or the world or God, but which is essentially nameless. It is at this point that we can believe Heidegger had come close to mysticism, and his reference to Meister Eckhart strengthens this belief.

But certainly the country path was leading back towards St Martin's church. I do not wish to appear to conscript Heidegger into the church, and we shall see that even his later writings are not specifically Christian, though they have a strong religious tone. But what can be stated as simply matter of fact is that when Heidegger died in 1976 his remains were interred in St Martin's churchyard and a requiem mass was celebrated in the church at the philosopher's request by his old friend and colleague, Fr Bernard Welte.

2

Being and Time (1)

In this chapter and in the one that follows, we shall be examining Heidegger's teaching as expressed in his book, *Being and Time*. We have already seen that this book was never completed. Nevertheless, it remains foundational for the development of Heidegger's philosophy and for an understanding of that philosophy. It cannot be stressed too much that *Being and Time* is not primarily a philosophical anthropology, though unfortunately the actual text, in the incomplete form in which Heidegger left it, is mainly taken up with the existential analytic conveying the impression that this is a man-centred philosophy, perhaps even the culmination of the subjectivist tendencies that have been at work in European philosophy for several centuries. But if we read the book carefully, we see that Heidegger's intention from the beginning was to attempt what might be called a 'general ontology' in which the analytic of *Dasein* would constitute only the first stage. Three years after the publication of *Being and Time*, Heidegger emphatically declared in his essay, *The Essence of Truth*, '[Man] is the more mistaken, the more exclusively he takes himself to be the measure of all things.'[1] Perhaps Sartre was right when he said that existentialism is a humanism, but this has nothing to do with Heidegger.[2]

The opening pages of *Being and Time* make it clear that Heidegger intends to revive the question of Being, that is to say, of Being in the widest sense: 'Our aim in the following treatise', he writes, 'is to work out the question of the meaning of Being' and he adds that 'our provisional aim is the interpretation of time as the horizon within which any understanding whatever of Being is possible'[3] There is no mention of *Dasein* here.

Heidegger was, of course, well aware that the question about the meaning of Being is not likely to be popular with philosophers of the present day, even if it excited the Greeks and continued to feature in European thinking at least until the time of Hegel. Various reasons are cited by Heidegger to account for the current neglect of the problem of Being, or even the suspicion that it is a pseudo-problem. It is said that 'being' is the most general of concepts, and must therefore be virtually empty of content and undefinable. This would indeed be the case if 'being' were a predicate like, say, 'redness' or 'materiality'. 'The universality of "being" is not that of a class or genus.' The point that 'being' is not a predicate had been made by Kant in his criticism of the ontological argument for God's existence, though Kant is not mentioned by Heidegger. But it does not need much reflection to realize that when one lists the predicates of anything, nothing is added to the description by saying that it is real or exists. To say that something exists is quite a different kind of assertion from saying it is red or material. Heidegger points out that in mediaeval ontology, the universality of 'being' led it to be designated a '*transcendens*,' going beyond even the most extensive generic concepts.

A further objection to pursuing the question of Being is that it is indefinable. If by definition we mean assigning something to a genus and then naming the specific difference that distinguishes it from other members of the genus, then this would no doubt follow from the alleged universality of 'being'. But may there be other ways of elucidating the meaning of a concept besides what was understood as 'definition' in traditional logic?

It may also be objected that the meaning of 'being' is self-evident. After all, we are continually using the verb 'to be' in one or other of its parts, and this surely shows that we already have an understanding of it. It may indeed be the case that we already have some understanding of what it means 'to be', but we are by no means clear about what we mean. Perhaps we have reflected far enough to have distinguished various meanings of, say, the word 'is': There is the 'is' of predication, the 'is' of identity, the 'is' of existence, and possibly many more. But we find it very difficult to bring any of these varieties of 'is' to clear understanding.

So it can hardly be denied that there is a problem here. We can hardly utter a sentence without using some part of the verb 'to be' and yet we confess our inability to say clearly what we mean by these 'being-words'. According to Aquinas, 'That which first falls under apprehension is "being" (*ens*), an understanding of which is included in all things whatsoever one apprehends.'⁴ Now, if this is the case, the way toward answering the question about the meaning of Being would seem to lie in clarifying and bringing to the highest possible level of intelligibility that understanding of being which, though not self-evident, is already present in varying degrees of intelligibility or obscurity in the human mind. We have seen in our first chapter that Heidegger believed that the *Dasein* in which the human mind participates is like a clearing in which Being comes to light. He believed that this had already been grasped by Parmenides in the dawn of philosophy when he linked thinking and being, for thinking cannot fail to be a thinking of Being, and it is this that establishes the peculiar link between *Dasein* and *Sein*. Perhaps this is the equivalent in Heideggerian terms of the biblical doctrine that the human being is made in the image of God. But Heidegger does not derive his view from the Bible, but from that saying of Parmenides which he interprets as meaning that the thinking of being is the same as Being. So we are pointed to *Dasein* as the locus where we must search for the meaning of Being.

As far as we human beings know, *Dasein* is the only being which asks the question about the meaning of Being, so even if we are still dubious about Heidegger's interpretation of the saying of Parmenides and about his assertion of an essential link between *Dasein* and *Sein* or Being in the widest sense, we might still be persuaded that just to have the possibility of raising the onto-logical question confers a peculiar ontological status on the questioner. There is already some understanding of Being here, for we do not ask about anything without already having some idea, however vague, of what we are asking about. I suppose a stone or a tree also has Being, but it would be bizarre to suppose that a stone or a tree has an understanding of Being or has any capacity for raising questions about Being.

Can we specify in more detail what it is that makes the

difference between *Dasein* and all the other beings that are encountered in the world? Heidegger mentions two distinguishing characteristics of *Dasein*. The first is that 'the essence of *Dasein* lies in its existence'.[5] Other entities have properties that are 'given' to them by 'nature', as we say, but *Dasein* has possibilities which it may either grasp or let slip. In Heidegger's view, this difference is so fundamental that he claims that the categories which we use in describing and defining things are not applicable to *Dasein*, for which it is necessary to work out a scheme of *existentialia*, that is to say, the basic possibilities of *Dasein*. This is simply an attempt to express in a more detailed and philosophical way the common-sense distinction which we all make between persons and things, or non-persons. The second distinguishing mark of *Dasein* mentioned by Heidegger is more difficult to pin down. It might be called the unique individuality that belongs to *Dasein*. Heidegger expresses it by saying that *Dasein* is in each case mine, or yours, or at any rate somebody's. One could also express this by saying that every *Dasein* is irreplaceable. If a copy of a book is destroyed, another copy will do just as well. But when this or that *Dasein* leaves the world, something unique has gone. This may be why we assign to any human life a value that cannot be measured.

But here we have to notice another peculiarity of the *Dasein*. This was hinted at when it was said that *Dasein* is constituted by possibilities, which may be grasped or may be let slip. Though *Dasein* is different and knows itself to be different from other entities, it has a tendency to see itself as just another item in the world. It seeks to shed responsibility for its being. It conforms to external pressures. In the Heideggerian terminology, it stands before two basic possibilities. It can be *authentic*, which means primarily just being its own self (the German word is *eigentlich*), or it can be *inauthentic* (*uneigentlich*) which means it has become a mere creature of fashion and convention, or a mere cog in the economic machine or a faceless unit in mass society. Perhaps few people attain to authenticity, and perhaps none are authentic all the time. Most of us settle for what Heidegger calls 'everyday' existence, and in the modern world that means following the same routines day after day and being like everyone else.

It is interesting to note that at this point in his exposition, Heidegger makes an important allusion to Christian theology.[6] He quotes Genesis 1.26 in the Septuagint version, 'And God said, "Let us make man in our image and likeness"', and he quotes also passages from both Calvin and Zwingli, to the effect that the creation of the human race was intended to be the beginning of a process in which man would 'transcend' (Calvin's word) toward God or 'be drawn' (Zwingli's expression) toward God because of the image in him. Heidegger's own comment is: 'In modern times, the Christian definition has been deprived of its theological character. But the idea of "transcendence" – that man is something that reaches beyond himself – is rooted in Christian dogmatics.'

But now we must turn to the details of Heidegger's account of the structure of *Dasein*. He presents us with a phenomenological analysis[7] in which he sets out the basic characteristics or *existentialia*. His starting-point is his insistence that *Dasein* must always be understood as Being-in-the-world. Near the beginning of this book, I pointed out that Heidegger is always trying to overcome the dichotomies or dualisms that have arisen in Western philosophy. These dualisms have usually arisen through the breaking up of an original unity. None of them is more annoying to Heidegger than the supposition that there might be a worldless subject which subsequently has to be related to an external world. Many epistemologists have talked as if this were the case, but Heidegger would blame them for having become involved in pseudo-problems. As soon as *Dasein* emerges into consciousness, it finds itself in a world. But what does it mean to be 'in' a world? It does not mean simply or even primarily to be *located* in a world. To understand the expression in that way is just an example of the *Dasein's* tendency to understand itself as another thing in the world. Being-in-the-world is 'dwelling' in the world, and 'dwelling' is a rich and complex relationship, far more than simply the spatial relationship of being located somewhere. Dwelling in the world means living in the closest interrelations with the world. It means being concerned with the world, deriving sustenance from the world, fashioning the world, perhaps tending for and preserving the world, even if we have performed this task very poorly. Although Heidegger was writing before people became so anxious about issues of the environment, it is interesting to note that he considers the world mainly as *Umwelt*, that is to say, 'surrounding world' or environment. Within that environment, we are constantly dealing with things of all kinds. But what is a 'thing'? Heidegger writes: 'The Greeks had an appropriate term for "things": *pragmata* – that is to say, that which one has to do with in one's concernful dealings (*praxeis*).'[8] Here we again see Heidegger trying to overcome a duality. When we speak of a 'thing', we usually think of a material 'object,' something just lying around, as it were, and the Greeks too, so we are told, came to think of things in that way. But in Heidegger's view, this 'objective' way of looking at things is an abstraction from an originally more concrete practical or pragmatic way. This is a point at which his concentration on *everyday* existence does bring us back to a more basic stance of the *Dasein* in which theory and practice have not yet been separated.

For everyday existence, the world is a world of work. In the first instance, things are seen not as objects for inspection but as items of equipment for *Dasein*'s tasks. This is obviously true of artefacts, such as a hammer. We understand the being of a hammer, so to speak, not by learning what it is made of, but by seeing someone using it in the act of hammering. Things are ready-to-hand (*zuhanden*) in the sense that we incorporate them into our activities. Something which merely confronts us as an object is said to be present-at-hand (*vorhanden*), but increasingly we bring even such things into the realm of equipment. The very stars become instruments for finding the way. The sun becomes our principal instrument for measuring time.

I did contrast Heidegger's view that *Dasein* is always already a Being-in-the-world with the view that there is a worldless subject which has to relate to a world, and I characterized the second of these views as subjectivist. But does not Heidegger's theory of the world as a vast system of equipment also indicate subjectivism? I do not think so, for in this case, *Dasein* is already wholly involved with the world in a reciprocal relationship. The fact that, on the everyday level, he sees this world as an instrumental system does not imply that this is a subjectivizing view. This is something like the anthropic principle recognized by cosmologists. For any world or universe to be seen as such, there must be some conscious being who so perceives it, and in the case of a human being, this perception can only be human. For us, at any rate, there is no God's eye view, and certainly there is no view from nowhere. It is, moreover, the point of view that gives the unity of what is perceived. No item of equipment can be understood by itself, and every such item implies others. Thus a pen has meaning only in relation to paper; this in turn implies writing, correspondence, a whole world of communication and likewise a world of learning and research. We see that 'world' is an *a priori* idea, already implied in the pragmatic understanding of things as interlocking instruments.

Heidegger of course is not denying the possibility of a more 'scientific' or theoretical concept of world. But he would argue that this is an abstraction from that more concrete understanding of world which arises out of the manifold relation to the world which belongs to *Dasein* as Being-in-the-world. *Dasein* is not primarily an observer of the world, but one who has been 'thrown' into the world and fated to dwell there. Theoretical knowledge is seen by Heidegger as a special but not privileged modification of Being-in-the-world.

But if anyone feels that Heidegger's account of the world in *Being and Time* is too heavily weighted toward the human exploitation of the world and too little appreciative of the world's intrinsic dignity and beauty, let him or her take comfort from the thought that probably Heidegger came to think in that way too, and in his later philosophy offered a richer view of the things of the world.

One other important point emerges from the understanding of world which has just been sketched out. Such a world must be a common world (*Mitwelt*). If a pen implies paper, it also implies the recipient of the letter. *Dasein* is a Being-with. Even a solitary *Dasein* is still essentially a Being-with. Heidegger is again distinguishing himself from those who might be called 'existentialists' and who tend to exalt the individual. Heidegger in this part of his book is close to Martin Buber, whose classic *I and*

Thou (*Ich und Du*) had been published in 1923, though Heidegger makes no mention of Buber. But he does distinguish between an authentic relationship which respects the person-hood of the other, and an inauthentic relationship in which there may be domination or possessiveness or the like. Most Being-with is of the inauthentic kind, and Heidegger spends considerable time portraying the dominance in mass society of the impersonal crowd, what he calls *das Man*, what in English we usually express by 'they,' as when we say, 'They say that there will be severe unemployment' or 'They are complaining about the selection of the Olympic team.' 'They' does not designate any particular group of people but simply reports some popular opinion or even a rumour. We are all victims of the 'they', indeed, when someone says 'I' he will very likely just be repeating what 'they' are saying.

We have seen that *Dasein*'s basic state is Being-in-the-world, and that this implies Being-with-others. We have also seen that the expression 'being in' is not to be understood in the sense of a bare location. The preposition 'in' conceals a rich multi-stranded relationship of 'dwelling' and might be best summed up by a word like 'concern' (*Besorgen*), the care (*Sorge*) which we have for things and which is analogous to the care we have for other *Dasein*s in Being-with, though Heidegger designates this care on the personal level by still another cognate term (*Fürsorge*), which may be translated 'solicitude'. The next step in the analysis is to probe more deeply into these relationships. Heidegger, however, reminds us yet again that the study of *Dasein* is not the primary aim of his work, but is undertaken as the 'fundamental ontology' on the way to answering the question about the meaning of Being.[9]

The first phenomenon discussed by Heidegger in this section of his work is designated by the German word *Befindlichkeit*. It is hard to find a good English equivalent. It means the condition in which one finds oneself at any given time. 'State-of-mind' was the translation which Edward Robinson and I used in our translation of *Being and Time*, and although this gets the meaning, it is not very satisfactory, especially in introducing the word 'mind' which has nothing corresponding to it in the German expression. In his discussion, Heidegger sometimes uses the word *Stimmung* to explain *Befindlichkeit*, and *Stimmung* would correspond to 'mood' or 'attunement' in English. Perhaps 'affective state' would be a useful translation. Our moods change quite often and we may not know why this happens, but Heidegger believes that they play an important part in disclosing *Dasein* to itself. It might be going too far to claim for moods a cognitive function, but they are evoked by the varying situations in which we find ourselves and they light up these situations for us, perhaps bringing to light features of the situation which could not be revealed by sense-perception alone. Heidegger gives as an illustration of such a mood an analysis of fear as the mode in which we become aware of a situation as threatening. Fear discloses to us the vulnerability of *Dasein*. When such a mood comes over someone, he or she is made aware of the sheer 'facticity' of *Dasein*, who, in Heidegger's language, finds himself 'thrown' into a world in which he is and has to be, yet without having chosen this existence and without knowing whence he has come or whither he is going.

Next Heidegger discusses understanding as another factor in the disclosedness of *Dasein*. State-of-mind and understanding are said to be equiprimordial in constituting *Dasein*'s disclosedness – 'a state-of-mind always has its understanding . . . and understanding always has its mood'[10] We have already seen how Heidegger tries to bridge the gap between practice and theory by claiming that understanding is in the first instance directed to the practical tasks of Being-in-the-world, and that theoretical understanding is derived from the practical use of understanding by a process of abstraction.

Whereas state-of-mind discloses *Dasein* as already thrown into a situation, understanding looks to the possibilities that lie ahead. The word which is perhaps most typical in Heidegger's exposition of understanding is 'project'. *Dasein* is constantly projecting, though Heidegger uses the expression so freely that one has to ask if he is quite consistent. *Dasein* projects itself, meaning, possibilities, even the world and the use of the word needs close scrutiny. We have already seen that, at the practical level, *Dasein* constructs the world with a view to the serviceability of things. But in the course of history, there has developed out of the practical understanding a theoretical understanding of the world, and a point may be reached where *Dasein* seeks an understanding simply out of the desire to know, even if there are no obvious practical advantages in knowing. However, it may be doubted if, on the one hand, there is any art or skill, even if performed tacitly, that does not imply some theory, and, on the other hand, whether there is any theoretical activity that does not have its practical aspects. Two years after the publication of *Being and Time*, Heidegger wrote *Kant and the Problem of Metaphysics*. The table of categories (that is to say, the fundamental concepts we employ in the understanding of the world) is, as devised by Kant, frankly theoretical and founded on logic. Kant himself was conscious of the distance that lies between these categories and the world of everyday experience. So he attempted what he called the 'schematism' of the categories. This, he claimed, is a work of the imagination, bringing the categories into time and so making them applicable to beings in time. According to Heidegger's reading, Kant in the first edition of *The Critique of Pure Reason* came very close to abandoning the traditional belief in timeless logic and timeless categories (in other words, he came close to anticipating Heidegger!) but in the second edition he fell back to the traditional point of view.

This is perhaps the place to introduce the subject of truth, though it comes somewhat later in the order of Heidegger's exposition. His remarks on the categories of Kant will have prepared us for his denial that there are any 'eternal truths.' He declares, 'the contention that there are "eternal truths" . . . belongs to those residues of Christian theology within philosophical thought which have not as yet been radically extruded.'[11]

This needs some further explanation. We have already come across some examples of the way in which Heidegger uses etymologies to appeal to what he believes to have been the original meanings of words in order to establish some point in his argument. He often uses this device in passages where truth is mentioned. In Greek, truth is *aletheia*. This word is a privative expression, meaning 'uncoveredness' or 'unconcealment'. We attain the truth when something is presented to us as it really is, without any concealment or distortion. Another point follows from this, that the locus of truth is not the proposition, but *Dasein*, who is in the truth, because *Dasein* is the clearing within which Being presents itself. Therefore, on this view, truth is not a property of propositions but an event in *Dasein*. Incidentally, one could argue that this understanding of truth was already to be found in the Gospel of John and likewise in the writings of Kierkegaard. Should Heidegger therefore not reject it as one of those residues of Christian theology that ought to be radically extruded from philosophy?

But leaving that question aside, we note what he says about Newton's laws of motion: 'These are true, only as long as *Dasein* is. Before there was any *Dasein*, there was no truth; nor will there be any after *Dasein* is no more. For in such a case, truth as disclosing, uncovering and uncoveredness, cannot be.' But this is not meant to suggest for a moment that truth is subjective, or that it can be made whatever we want it to be. In *The Essence of Truth* (from which I earlier quoted Heidegger as saying that man is the more mistaken, the more exclusively he takes himself to be the measure of all things), truth is linked with freedom, the freedom of letting-be; we perceive the truth of something when we let it be what it really is.

We have seen that it is Heidegger's policy to bring together what has been, as he believes, erroneously separated in the history of philosophy. A further example of this is his insistence that understanding and sense-perception belong together. What we see is never just a coloured patch, but, let us say, a house or a lake; what we hear is not a bare sound but, say, the singing of a bird or the screeching of brakes. As he had already said in his lectures of 1925 (*The History of the Concept of Time*), 'Even simple perception, which is often called sense-perception, is clearly intrinsically pervaded by categorial intuition.'[12]

What has just been said is related closely also to Heidegger's doctrine that all understanding includes interpretation. Understanding always has an 'as-structure', which means that we see the things of the environment *as* doors, or *as* tables or *as* whatever they may be. They already have meanings. There is not only an as-structure, but a fore-structure as well. We never come to anything with a blank or presuppositionless mind, but always with a pre-understanding, already accepted ways of seeing, conceiving and knowing.

Language (*Sprache*), or rather discourse (*Rede*) is another basic *existentiale* discussed by Heidegger, and we have seen his fascination with etymologies and the history of words, which he often takes to be revelatory of *Dasein* and even of Being. But the fuller development of his philosophy of language came only later in his career, and we shall therefore defer discussion of it for the present.

We pass on therefore to consider another phenomenon which belongs to everyday existence – the phenomenon which Heidegger calls 'falling' (*Verfallen*). He tells us that the word 'does not express any negative evaluation'[13] but points to *Dasein*'s absorption into the everyday environment, especially into the 'they', the inauthentic Being-with-others in which individual differences are suppressed and people live alike, talk alike and think alike. This is a state of affairs which is even more obvious in our time than it was when Heidegger was writing, due mainly to the vastly increased influence of the media, especially television. The levelling process has, of course, gone just as far in supposedly liberal and democratic societies as it did in societies that were overtly totalitarian.

But why, it may be asked, does Heidegger tell us that the word '*Verfallen*' does not express any negative evaluation? This verb in German does suggest not only deterioration but even some kind of corruption. Heidegger, however, seems set to evade making any ethical judgment, and this is typical. When, near the beginning of his book, he introduced the terms 'authentic' and 'inauthentic', he claimed that 'the inauthenticity of *Dasein* does not signify any "less" Being or any "lower" degree of Being'.[14] Now when he talks of a 'falling' of *Dasein* (to use the most neutral translation of *Verfallen*) he is certainly aware that such language is bound to suggest to the reader a comparison with the theological doctrine of a fall of man and original sin. He does in fact say in one place that *ontically* (that is to say, actually), he makes no judgment as to whether human beings are in a state of corruption or of wholeness or of grace.[15] The phenomenon of falling, like the other existential phenomena described in Heidegger's analysis, is exhibited as a possibility rather than an actuality. So in shying away from ethical judgments Heidegger may be merely trying to preserve the neutrality of the phenomenological method. He may also be trying to distance himself from any theological implications. But one might have expected that in discussing 'falling' or fallenness even as existential possibility, it is clearly admitted that it is in some important sense a 'falling short', an ontological parallel to the theological concept of sin.

These suspicions are strengthened when we consider some of Heidegger's detailed descriptions of what may be called the symptoms of falling. One of them is 'idle talk' (*Gerede*), the chattering which passes for conversation in much of everyday relations with one another. Here too Heidegger tells us that the expression 'idle talk' is not to be taken in a disparaging sense, though unquestionably the expression does have disparaging connotations in both its German and English forms. And when one reads what Heidegger says about it, the sense of disparagement increases. Idle talk is a perversion of speech, in which things are covered up rather than revealed. Other symptoms of falling are described as curiosity, ambiguity, tranquilizing and alienation. The last named is perhaps of special importance. *Dasein* has the possibility of falling away from itself. This does not, of course, mean that it becomes merely a thing, but it surrenders or compromises its authentic Being-in-the-world as that entity which is not just another innerworldly item but that peculiar entity in which existence precedes essence and makes possible a measure of autonomy and creativity. Falling takes place when *Dasein* flees from itself and from its possibilities and responsibilities. It does so by losing itself in the anonymity and irresponsibility of the 'they' and in its restless but tranquillizing concern with the things that surround it. This is the forgetting of Being, and in Heidegger's understanding of the matter, it is the way to nihilism.

At this point, we must gather together the various insights into the constitution of *Dasein* that we have found in accompanying Heidegger along the path of his existential analytic. We remind ourselves that we are looking chiefly for a philosophy of time and history so that we can assess its implications for religious faith, especially Christian faith. It might seem that so far we have not found much that is relevant to our quest. We did, of course, take note of Heidegger's unusual understanding of truth, in particular, his denial that there are any 'eternal truths' and his contention that the locus of truth lies not in propositions but in the being of *Dasein* itself. But apart from that, have we come any distance toward seeing how time and history have, as Heidegger has claimed, a key role for the interpretation of human life and of reality generally – how time is, in the Heideggerian expression, the 'horizon' for any possible interpretation of Being?

Because the human mind cannot grasp everything at once and must always proceed seriatim, Heidegger has set out his understanding of *Dasein* in a long series of phenomenological analyses – existence and essence, individuality, Being-in-the-world, concern, dwelling, Being-with-others, state-of-mind, understanding, falling and so on. But we remember that one of his endeavours in philosophy was to restore unities that have been broken up. *Dasein* is a unity which may indeed be broken up for the purpose of achieving an understanding of its constitution, but in this process we should not lose sight of the unity. It is as if we have in front of us many pieces of a jigsaw. We have been taken through the various items that can be discerned in the everyday existence of *Dasein*, but we can only gain a proper grasp of them when we see them in their original unity. The First Division therefore of *Being and Time* ends with a chapter in which Heidegger restores the balance by showing *Dasein* as a unity which embraces all the diverse phenomena which he has analysed. He remarks: 'To be sure, the constitution of the structural whole and its everyday kind of Being, is phenomenally so *manifold* that it can easily obstruct our looking at the whole as such phenomenologically in a way which is *unified*.'[16] But how do we grasp this unity? Would we need an architect's plan to put all the pieces correctly together?

Heidegger's answer to that question is startling, but quite typical. It is in the mood of anxiety that we glimpse the unity of *Dasein*. We have seen that state-of-mind or mood is a basic way in which *Dasein* is disclosed to itself. Anxiety, in Heidegger's view, is the state-of-mind which is most radically disclosive of *Dasein*. We shall meet this concept of anxiety again, but for the present we note that it differs from fear in having no definite object. It is more like a vague *malaise*. It is a mood which people may experience only rarely, but it lights up the fragility and finitude of *Dasein*.

In Heidegger's terminology, it exhibits the unity of *Dasein* as *care*. It is care that gathers up the various phenomena that have been examined. *Dasein* understands itself as possibility thrown into the world, it comes face to face with its being free for the authenticity of its being, being free for the freedom of choosing itself and taking hold of itself.[17]

It is now that we are in a position to see the fundamental importance of time and temporality. If the being of *Dasein* can be summed up as care, the conclusion seems to be that *Dasein* is not an enduring substance but a temporal structure, and that would seem to be something quite insubstantial. To quote Heidegger: 'The fundamental ontological characteristics of this entity are existentiality, facticity and being-fallen. These existential characteristics are not pieces belonging to something composite, one of which might sometimes be missing; but there is woven together in them a primordial context which makes up the totality of the structural whole which we are seeking.'

Of the three ontological characteristics mentioned by Heidegger, existentiality relates to understanding, which projects *Dasein*'s possibilities ahead of itself into the future. Facticity relates to state-of-mind, the disclosure to *Dasein* that it is already thrown into a situation, that it has a past which has somehow brought it to its present. Being-fallen is the present absorption of *Dasein* into its world and the 'they'. This unitary yet manifold structure is summed up by Heidegger in what must surely rank as perhaps the most cumbrous and inelegant sentence ever devised by him: 'The Being of *Dasein* means ahead-of-itself-Being-already-in-(the-world) as Being-alongside (entities encountered within-the-world).'[18]

Time and temporality have now come into the foreground of our discussion. But up till now we have been thinking of *Dasein* in its everyday and largely inauthentic mode of being. So now we must turn our attention to the Second Division of *Being and Time*, where Heidegger seeks to show *Dasein* in its authentic Being.

3

Being and Time (2)

We have seen how Heidegger's phenomenological analysis of *Dasein* has led to the concept of care as a comprehensive description of *Dasein*'s basic ontological structure, and we have seen that care itself has a temporal basis. *Dasein*, as understanding, projects its possibilities for being into the future; it does so as an entity that already finds itself in a situation which has been determined by the past; and in the moment between past and future, it is distracted by and absorbed in the present demands of routine existence in the world – an existence which is described as 'fallen,' because it tends to deprive *Dasein* of its distinctive existence and treats this entity as just another item within the world.

But although Heidegger claimed at the beginning of his existential analytic that we should study *Dasein* in its everyday existence, he now indicates that this procedure can bring only a provisional result. He reminds us again at the beginning of Division Two of his work that our quest is the meaning of 'Being' in general, and that the analysis of *Dasein*, as that entity which raises the question of Being and has already some implicit understanding of Being, is only the preliminary to the main inquiry.[1] It is therefore vital that, before we go further, we make sure that our understanding of *Dasein* is as adequate as we can make it.

He acknowledges that the analysis which has resulted in the description of *Dasein* as care is inadequate in two respects, and must be repeated and deepened. The first failure is that the analysis so far has dealt with only episodes in the existence of *Dasein*. But *Dasein* in its entirety comprises the whole temporal structure that lies between birth and death. Can we find a way of grasping *Dasein* in its entirety? The second failure is that we have been studying *Dasein* in its everyday manifestations, and such everyday existence is largely characterized by inauthenticity, that is to say, *Dasein* is not really itself, not really the creative centre that it has the possibility to become, but a product of the dominant 'they', tranquilized and alienated. So we have to look anew at *Dasein*. To see *Dasein* in its completeness means that we have to turn our attention to death, which, so to speak, closes the account for every *Dasein*. To see *Dasein* in its authenticity means that we have to turn our attention to conscience as that structure in *Dasein* directing it to the realization of its existential possibilities.

To make death a major philosophical theme was certainly a revolutionary step. Did it announce the appearance of a new nihilism? Richard Kroner recalls the shock which Heidegger's teaching caused in 1927: 'What was most fascinating and startling to me was not so much his metaphysical conception of Being, but rather his thoughts about death and mortality. These thoughts seemed to be in the very centre of his whole discussion. When I was a student, the Germans talked and wrote much about "philosophy of life", which Nietzsche especially had popularized, and it had been widely accepted in non-academic literary circles. Our university professors despised and severely criticized such a popular philosophy, telling us that it had no scientific value but merely stirred the emotions, and that a serious analysis could easily refute it. Heidegger, however, had transformed this philosophy of life into a philosophy of death and had furnished it with the solid defence of a critical method, thus giving it academic respectability. In this new attire, the formerly rejected philosophy of life demanded the greatest attention and the most careful study.'[2]

Is Kroner correct in claiming that this philosophy of death demands 'our most careful study'? Or is it simply one man's subjective and emotional reaction to the human situation? Our answer to such questions will depend on how we answer more general questions. Is philosophy a purely intellectual exercise, to be carried out in abstraction from the emotional and volitional elements in human nature by techniques of reasoning alone? Or does philosophizing have a broader basis – at least, such philosophizing as takes for its theme the question of Being? Must not this kind of philosophizing be rooted in total human existence? Or, to put it in another way, are we disclosed to ourselves as existents who are always already in a world, with which we are concerned and involved in multifarious ways, rather than mere observers, so that it is out of this whole situation that we must seek after such understanding of Being as may be possible?

But let us see how Heidegger attempts a phenomenology of death and how he integrates it into his philosophy. He is not interested in death as a natural phenomenon. That belongs to biology, and is a fate which human beings share with animals. Neither is Heidegger going to engage in any speculative problems about the possibility of life beyond death. This is in line with his belief that phenomenology, like the natural sciences, is neutral or even, in a methodological sense, atheistic. 'The this-worldly ontological interpretation of death,' he tells us, 'takes precedence over any ontical other-worldly speculation.'[3] His aim, in a phenomenology of death, is to ask how it enters into the being of *Dasein*, and what it tells us about *Dasein*.

But is any phenomenology of death at all possible? In the analysis of everyday existence, Heidegger examined such phenomena as understanding, affectives states, speech, anxiety, concern, solicitude and so on. These all belong to daily experience, we know them from our continuous participation in them and from reflection upon them, and it is therefore possible to carry out the descriptive analyses that we find in the earlier chapters of *Being and Time*. But with death it is different. This is not an everyday experience on which we can ponder, but the end of all experience. Heidegger's hope of grasping the *Dasein* in its completeness from birth to death seems to be illusory, for even as it reaches completeness, *Dasein* ceases to be.

Can we overcome the difficulty by observing the deaths of other people? We can see them ceasing to exist. But then we are seeing death only as a natural event, happening 'out there', so to speak. We are not experiencing it as something belonging to our *Dasein*. But Heidegger does draw one positive characteristic of death from the failure to have access to the death of others. We remember that in his first descriptions of *Dasein*, he mentioned the rather mysterious point that each *Dasein* is always someone's own. It has a uniqueness, individuality, irreplaceability, difficult to describe, yet central to each *Dasein*. This particularity is prominent especially in relation to death. No one can die for another, in the sense of performing that other's death for him or her. One may go to death on behalf of another, and in that way 'save' the other's life by postponing that person's death. But such a 'dying for', according to Heidegger, 'can never signify that the other has thus had his death taken away in even the slightest degree'.[4] So the unsuccessful project of reaching an understanding of death by observing the death of others at least brings us to the recognition that death is, perhaps in a unique way, *untransferable*.

Perhaps there is some analogy that might light up the phenomenon of death. We think of death as the end of *Dasein*. But it is not an additional event, coming at the end of life. It belongs to the very being of *Dasein*. Heidegger asks whether death might be compared to the ripening of a fruit. This is not something that gets added to the fruit, but a specific way in which the fruit *is*. But Heidegger at once acknowledges that the analogy soon breaks down, for while ripeness is the fulfilment of the fruit, death often comes when the deceased has not fulfilled his or her potentialities, or it may delay until the person is broken down. But here again something positive – or so it is claimed – emerges from the failure of this analogical attempt to penetrate to the existential significance of death. Death (and this is surely paradoxical) is the ultimate possibility for *Dasein*, the possibility *that cannot be outstripped*.

I have used the word 'paradoxical' for Heidegger's view of death, for it is not quite clear whether he is simply recommending realism in the face of death, that is, recommending that *Dasein* acknowledges that there is a cut-off point to existence and that one's choices must take this into account; or whether there is a more sinister, even nihilistic, exaltation of death in the view he recommends.

The question is not clearly answered in Heidegger's further remarks on the subject. For he now traces in death the familiar temporal pattern. As possibility, death belongs to the future. It is indeed my capital possibility, the one in front of which all other possibilities lie and in relation to which they must be evaluated. Here Heidegger differs from his self-styled disciple, Sartre, who asserts that death is not a possibility in the existential sense, but the cancellation of all possibilities and the final absurdity that reveals the meaninglessness of life. Heidegger does not go so far as that, indeed, he could be understood as teaching that it is precisely death that enables *Dasein* to achieve a meaningful pattern within a limited lifespan. What is important is to live even now in anticipatory awareness of death as one's untransferable and uttermost possibility, and this might be understood as a kind of secularized and individualized eschatology.

If death relates to the future as possibility, it relates also to what has been as an element in *Dasein*'s facticity. Every *Dasein* is already thrown into death. We can take it over passively or we can appropriate it actively, but we cannot escape it. It is the most certain event in *Dasein*'s existence, yet along with its certainty goes an indefiniteness – it can happen at any moment.

So death is also, in a sense, present. It is already accessible, as thrown possibility, and is accessible to the existential analytic. A 'fallen' or inauthentic existence dwells, as we have seen in the present, but it covers up from itself the present possibility of death. Especially in modern society, mention of death is avoided or is veiled in euphemistic language. But that is just one more symptom of *Dasein*'s reluctance to face the truth of its own being.

Heidegger urges us to anticipate death, not in the sense of rushing upon death in any suicidal way, but in the sense of a 'being-toward-death', a clear-sighted acceptance of human finitude. It means living in awareness of the steady presence of death. Here again we meet the mood of anxiety. 'The state-of-mind which can hold open the utter and constant threat to itself arising from *Dasein*'s ownmost individualized being is anxiety (*Angst*).'[5] This enables *Dasein* to escape from its fallenness and take upon itself its own authentic being. 'Anticipation reveals to *Dasein* its lostness in the they-self, and brings it face to face with the possibility of being itself . . . in an impassioned *freedom toward death*.'[6] These words mark the emotional climax of *Being and Time*, and perhaps their Promethean quality marks also his furthest departure from Christianity or any religious position in the direction of a 'metaphysic of rebellion' comparable to that of Albert Camus, though of course the latter was more of a literary figure than a philosopher in any serious sense.

These last remarks about Heidegger's distancing his thought from its earlier Christian associations are confirmed when we go on to the second phase in his deepening of the existential analytic, namely, when he describes *Dasein* in its authentic as opposed to its everyday mode of existence. Inauthenticity is not an inescapable fate for *Dasein*. 'Inauthenticity characterizes a kind of being into which *Dasein* can divert itself and has for the most part always diverted itself; but *Dasein* does not necessarily and constantly have to divert itself into this kind of being.'[7] The way of escape is willingness to listen to conscience (*Gewissen*). Conscience is still another way in which *Dasein* is disclosed to itself. As Heidegger describes it, conscience is like a call. It calls *Dasein* out of the self-deceptions of its fallen condition into a clear-sighted acceptance of its true situation as the finite existent already thrown into death – an acceptance of its 'freedom for death', to recall the phrase we have already met.

From where does this call of conscience come? It is not just the voice of society that we hear, not a superego imposed by parents or teachers. In fact, the call of conscience summons us away from the judgments of the 'they'. Nor is conscience the voice of God, and we need not suppose there is anything supernatural about it. Conscience arises from *Dasein* itself. *Dasein* is summoned by its own potentiality for authentic existing. 'In conscience, *Dasein* calls itself.'[8]

To listen to the call of conscience is to accept one's responsibility for one's existence. But to accept this responsibility is at the same time to become guilty. Heidegger's argument is.somewhat obscure at this point. He conceives guilt (*Schuld*) as meaning primarily 'debt'. *Dasein* is always guilty or indebted in the sense that it lags behind its own possibilities. It is not the ground of its own being but has been thrown into being. There is therefore a negation or nullity in the very constitution of *Dasein*. It is never the master of its own being, yet it is responsible for that being. This seems to indicate that there is some fundamental contradiction in *Dasein*, and again one has to wonder whether at this stage in his thinking Heidegger had come very close to Sartre's position that man is a 'useless passion',[9] a being of great possibilities which he is impotent to fulfil.

This, of course, is a point at which the existential analytic might have taken a religious turn. In Paul and in many other Christian writers, the sense of human weakness was a prelude to faith and reliance on divine grace. But there is nothing of this in *Being and Time*. The human being, as *Dasein* or being-in-the-world, is thrown into existence and at the same time into death, and has no resources other than his own. Later, of course, we shall find Heidegger explicitly dissociating himself from Sartre and from the type of humanism which makes man the measure of all things. Even at this stage, he may have been moving in another direction, and we have noted that only three years after the appearance of *Being and Time*, he was questioning the view that the human being is the ultimate judge.[10] But if we confine our attention to what is said in *Being and Time*, it can be freely acknowledged that Sartre can hardly be blamed for reading the book in the way that he did. We have already noted what I have called the 'emotional climax' in which Heidegger talks of an 'impassioned freedom for death'. After he has explored the characteristics of an authentic existence to which *Dasein* is called by conscience, there is another emotional passage in which an 'anticipatory resoluteness' in the face of death is represented as not just a grim resignation but a Promethean joy in the struggle: 'Along with the sober anxiety which brings us face to face with our individualized potentiality-for-being, there goes an unshakable joy in this possibility.'[11]

Heidegger's aim in discussing death and then conscience was to deepen the existential analysis of *Dasein* that had been worked out in the earlier chapters of *Being and Time*. What then is this further and supposedly more primordial interpretation of *Dasein*'s being to which we have been led? In a sense, there is nothing new or surprising about it, for it has all been sketched out already in the preceding discussions. It will be remembered that at the end of Division One of Heidegger's book, care was said to be the inclusive concept that sums up the being of *Dasein*. But care itself was shown to have a threefold structure: it comprises understanding, by which *Dasein* projects itself into the future; it comprises also those moods or affective states which disclose to *Dasein* the situation into which it finds itself already thrown as a result of past conditions; and finally it comprises fallenness, understood as *Dasein*'s present lostness in the inauthenticity of the 'they' and of routine existence. That interpretation of *Dasein* has been supplemented by the discussion of death and the call for anticipatory resoluteness. The entire picture brings into prominence the essentially temporal character of *Dasein*. This particular being which we ourselves are and which we have been studying as a preliminary to taking up the question of the meaning of Being as such is a temporal structure. What makes care possible is temporality, and so temporality is the phenomenon to which Heidegger has led us as the clue in the first instance to the understanding of the nature of *Dasein* including our own human existence, and then, so he hoped, as the clue to the even more ambitious question about the meaning of Being in general.

The emphasis on time and temporality, and therefore on history which is the temporality of communities, that is to say, of *Dasein* as Being-with, is a central feature of Heidegger's philosophy, but also marks a breach with much of the philosophical tradition. In that tradition, the self was usually thought to be a substance of some kind, perhaps a spiritual or immaterial substance, but nevertheless a substance. To deny substantiality to the self and to interpret it as a temporal structure would seem to rob it of claims to permanence. What is even more startling in Heidegger's philosophy is that Being as such appears to be temporal, and such a view is almost inevitable if one takes *Dasein* as the clue to the meaning of Being, and holds that *Dasein* is through and through temporal. One commentator remarks, 'Perhaps the most radical claim that Heidegger makes is that ontology has an essentially temporal character.'[12] But just how the temporality of *Dasein* relates to, let us say, the time of physics is left unclear by Heidegger, as we shall see in due course. After all, he did decide that there is no direct path from the analysis of *Dasein*'s being to the general question of Being.

Returning then to Heidegger's treatment of temporality as the basic interpretation of *Dasein*, there is a very important point to be noted. When we think of time, we generally assign to it three 'dimensions', if we may call them such – past, present and future. As we commonly visualize it, time is a series of successive 'nows'. Each 'now' is a fleeting moment, which arrives from the future and then slips into the past. We also tend to think that only what *is* now is real; the future is not yet real while the past is no longer real. But Heidegger rejects this common understanding of time. Like so many other things, it has been objectified or reified, as if these successive moments were so many things, present-at-hand. Objectified time is not the time we know at first hand in our experience of being-in-the-world. The objectified moments are all external to one another, but this is not the case in time as experienced by *Dasein*.

In *Dasein*'s time or temporality, the three dimensions (Heidegger prefers to call them 'ecstases') of past, present and future are internally related. The past enters into the future and the future into the past; both past and future help to constitute the present, which is not just a knife-edge between them but an appreciable span of duration. We have already seen examples of these internal relations in earlier analyses. The past, as facticity, still is to some extent determining the present and the future. So we find Heidegger uses sometimes the perfect tense rather than a simple past tense, for the perfect refers to an action which continues into the present or has its effects in the present, as distinct from a tense which treats an action as simply past. In a similar fashion, our projects, though they refer to the future, were formed in time that is now past and we are still engaged on them.

As mentioned above, the relation between this time of *Dasein* and what may be called 'clock-time' is somewhat obscure, and this is not surprising since time is one of the great mysteries. Likewise, the relation of time to space is not clear. Physicists talk of 'space-time' and sometimes of time as a 'fourth dimension', but time is not another dimension of the same order as length, breadth and thickness. It is peculiar in respect of its irreversibility, and this holds in human experience as well as in the surrounding world. There is an interesting note which Heidegger introduces into his discussion of time and in which he tentatively suggests a relation between *Dasein*'s temporality and God's. 'The fact that the traditional conception of "eternity" as signifying the "standing now" (*nunc stans*) has been drawn from the ordinary way of understanding time and has been defined with an orientation toward the idea of "constant" presence-at-hand, does not need to be discussed in detail. If God's eternity can be "construed" philosophically, then it may be understood only as a more primordial temporality which is "infinite". Whether the way afforded by the *via negationis et eminentiae* is a possible one, remains to be seen.'[13]

No less than three kinds of time seem to be mentioned in this last paragraph: the time or temporality of *Dasein*, world-time, and the time or temporality of God. We have seen that the temporality of *Dasein* is the span that stretches between birth and death. Heidegger tells us that this is not an empty slot of time into which a *Dasein* can be inserted, but that the *Dasein* 'stretches itself', suggesting that *Dasein* somehow generates its time, so that Heidegger might be thought to share with Kant the belief that time is a form imposed by consciousness on our intuitions of the material world. *Dasein*'s time is determined primarily by practical considerations – a time to get up, a time to go to work, and so on. But since *Dasein* is a being-with-others, individual times have to be correlated, and *Dasein* finds itself already in a world in which there is something like an objective time, regulated by the sun and the seasons. Although Heidegger does not raise the question, perhaps this world-time too was not already there 'waiting' for a world to begin a history within it, but, as modern science (and Augustine!) tell us, time began with the world and is in some sense generated by the world. Finally Heidegger's note compels us to ask about God's time, though I suppose that when Heidegger raised this question, he did so in a purely hypothetical way. But he seems clearly to be rejecting the notion that God is 'eternal' in the sense of 'timeless' or 'supratemporal'. God, like *Dasein* is temporal, but his temporality is said to be 'more primordial' than ours and also to be 'infinite'. So it does not seem to be claimed that God is within time (*innerzeitig*). Likewise *Dasein* is not within time, though essentially temporal. There is a parallel here between *Dasein*'s relation to time and its relation to the world. *Dasein* is always a being-in-the-world, but not another item or thing belonging to the world. So we may interpret Heidegger to mean that, if there is a God, he is temporal (and we shall see later some of the consequences of this), but that his temporality is something which he generates, not a medium more ultimate than himself.

Mention of a shared time and the need for clocks and calendars brings us to consider that specific form of temporal existence which we call history. *Dasein* does not exist as an isolated individual but in varying degrees of solidarity with others. Even one's most personal decisions are liable to be upset or overruled by major events occurring in the society of which one is a member, for instance, the outbreak of a war may completely alter a person's career.

When we talk about 'history', we are using an ambiguous word. In English, the most obvious ambiguity is that between 'history' as the stream of public events in time, and 'history' as the study of these events. In German, the ambiguity can be avoided. For 'history' as the stream of happening, one may use the word *Geschichte*, derived from the verb *geschehen*, 'to happen'. For 'history' as the study of historical happening, there is available the word *Historie*. Heidegger makes use of this distinction, but he points out that the term *Geschichte*, 'history' in the sense of the stream of events, has itself a variety of meanings. It is perhaps used most commonly of events that have happened in the past. It is used also of articles that have survived from the past when we say, for instance, that an ancient coin is a piece of history. Quite commonly too, we use the word 'history' and its derivatives for events brought about by human agency as distinct from events arising from natural causes. Thus, a battle is a historical event while a storm is a natural event, though the latter might qualify as a historical event if it affected the course of humanly originated events – an example would be the storm which is said to have scattered the ships of the Spanish Armada.

The point just made is taken by Heidegger to mean that what is primarily historical is always *Dasein* and that things, whether ready-to-hand or merely present-at-hand are only secondarily historical, through an association with *Dasein*. Artefacts in a museum, for instance, are called historical, but they are so only because they were once part of the totality of equipment that was ready-to-hand to *Dasein* in a world that is no longer. 'Manifestly', says Heidegger, '*Dasein* can *never* be past, not because *Dasein* is non-transient, but because essentially it can never be present-at-hand. Rather, if it is, it exists. A *Dasein* which no longer exists is not past, in the ontologically strict sense; it is rather "having-been-there." '[14]

Now, if *Dasein* is the primary historical, then what was said earlier about the temporality of *Dasein* must apply also to its historicality, for history is a specific form of temporality. Just as *Dasein* is to be understood in terms of *existentialia*, not of categories applicable to things, so it must be in historical studies, for example, historical causation is distinct from natural causation. Similarly, just as *Dasein*'s temporality is not a series of discrete 'nows', so in history the dimensions of past, present and future are internally related. Some paradoxical conclusions follow from these remarks. Thus history, in the sense of historical studies, is not so much concerned with the past as with the future, and not so much with facts as with possibilities. History goes into the past to discover the authentic possibilities of *Dasein*, so as to project these possibilities into the future. This is the act which Heidegger calls repetition or retrieval (*Wiederholung*). Perhaps this explains why many great statesmen have also been keen students of history; or why religious renewals have often been the result of a return to sources; or why Heidegger himself in his philosophical quest for the meaning of Being goes back to the fragmentary utterances of such presocratic thinkers as Heraclitus and Parmenides. But the notion of repetition or retrieval does raise a serious question. In laying so much stress on the paradigmatic role of great moments in the past, is he ruling out the possibility of great creative departures in the future? We have come nowadays to accept, at least subconsciously, the idea that knowledge is constantly being enlarged by new discoveries. To some extent, most people have embraced a belief in progress, a belief fostered by the constant advances of the natural sciences. Admittedly, one would have to say that outside of the natural sciences there is not much evidence of progress. Have people today made any moral advance beyond the peoples of earlier times? Those who have lived through the time of world wars and of the death camps of central and eastern Europe would find it hard to claim that progress has been made. Would it not be equally difficult to claim any progress in philosophy and religion, which between them have a powerful influence in shaping morality? Heidegger seems to believe that in these areas it is the beginning that is great and from then on there is a tendency to deterioration. Certainly the whole notion of a steady and universal progress, popular in the nineteenth century, has become much more dubious by the end of the twentieth. So bringing again the great possibilities disclosed in the past and making them present may quite probably be a sound policy in facing the future. But it does seem to suggest that *Dasein*'s highest possibilities have already been disclosed and that therefore the future of *Dasein* will not be an unlimited transcendence but the continuing discovery and rediscovery of the *Dagewesen* (*Dasein* that has been).

Does this suggest a comparison with Nietzsche's doctrine of the eternal recurrence of the same? Certainly Heidegger found much to interest and even fascinate him in Nietzsche's philosophy and wrote a lengthy work on Nietzsche, expounding but also criticizing his teaching.[15] When he was writing the sections of *Being and Time* which we are presently considering, Heidegger must have felt some affinity to Nietzsche. Is not his own view that *Dasein* must gain authenticity through its own resoluteness in being free for death reminiscent of Nietzsche's claim that God is dead and that yet this is a price worth paying if it allows man to take control of his own destiny?

Heidegger does in fact explicitly introduce Nietzsche in the course of his discussion of history in *Being and Time*. He refers to a volume of essays by Nietzsche, known in English as *Thoughts out of Season*, in German as *Unzeitmässige Betrachtungen*, where Nietzsche distinguishes three different ways of writing history. Like Heidegger, Nietzsche was interested in applying historical knowledge to the problems of living in the present. The first of his three types of history is what he calls 'monumental' history. In this kind of history, the great or 'monumental' achievements of the past serve as an inspiration for the present and the future. This is the type of historical retrieval that is of special interest to Heidegger, and it has also been important in religion and theology, where great revelatory events of the past are renewed and even re-enacted in story and ceremony. But Nietzsche's two other forms of history, the 'antiquarian' and the 'critical' are also recognized by Heidegger. The three together are approximately correlated with his own three ecstases of temporality, while the exploration of the past in order to criticize the present and to come to terms with the future are taken as further confirmation of the internal relations holding among past, present and future. Heidegger also relates his views on history to those of Wilhelm Dilthey who in the generation before Heidegger had attempted to construct a distinct methodology for the human sciences.

Heidegger's views on these matters are somewhat obscurely summed up in his own words as follows: 'Only an entity which, in its being, is essentially *futural* so that it is free for its death and can let itself be thrown back on its factical "there" by shattering itself against death – that is to say, only an entity which, as futural, is equiprimordially in the process of *having-been*, can, by handing down to itself the possibility it has inherited, take over its thrownness and be *in the moment of vision* for "its time". Only authentic temporality, which is at the same time finite, makes possible something like fate, that is to say, authentic historicality.'[16]

Some readers may be puzzled or even upset by the appearance in this quotation of the word 'fate'. In the same part of *Being and Time* appears a related word which may be even more disturbing, the word 'destiny'. The relation between the two words is more obvious in German than it is in English. The two words in German are *Schicksal* and *Geschick*. What is common to both of them is the syllable -schick-. That syllable is from the verb, *schicken*, 'to send'. A fate and likewise a destiny is not something that arises from our own choice but is *sent* to us. As Heidegger uses the terms, fate (*Schicksal*) is sent to the individual, destiny (*Geschick*) is sent to society or the nation or some other collectivity. So it would seem that history, in Heidegger's view, is not simply the outcome of human decisions and actions. Who or what, then, does the sending? Is the fate or destiny unavoidable?

In the English-speaking world, talk of fate or destiny is unusual. Some people may accept that human beings do not entirely determine the course of history but they would be more likely to talk of God or Providence than of fate and destiny. Sometimes these words have been used, but they arouse suspicion. In the nineteenth century (and perhaps among some people even today) there was an idea common in the United States called 'manifest destiny'. It was the belief that the United States is a model society with the mission of spreading its ethos and institutions throughout the world. Other nations, however, might see this as an illegitimate expansionism. Although the British did not talk of a 'manifest destiny', there were probably many who believed that the British Empire had a civilizing mission, though to colonial peoples the Empire may have seemed simply an imperialist power.

So what had Heidegger in mind when he talked of fate and destiny? Whence comes the 'sending'? We have already met the idea of throwness. *Dasein* did not create itself and it did not choose to exist. There is a sense therefore in which *Dasein* is sent into life and at the same time into death. Is the sender quite anonymous? A Christian would say that God is the sender. Heidegger does not say that, and at the time when he was writing *Being and Time*, he was determined to keep God out of his descriptions. Does it matter very much whether we say 'God' or use only the vague expression 'fate'? Perhaps it does not matter very much when we are talking about individuals, but when we go on to talk of the 'destinies' of great masses of people, we are on dangerous ground. The destiny of the German people was one of the driving ideas in National Socialism, and it was not a destiny of which God, if understood in Christian terms, could have approved. If one asks, 'What was there in Heidegger's philosophy that might have made him sympathetic to National Socialism?' I think the answer must be, his idea of history and destiny, as seen in the context of Germany in the years around 1930. But as has been said above[17] a discussion of these questions must be deferred for the present. Unfortunately too, Heidegger's own discussion of time and history breaks off abruptly, for *Being and Time* was never finished.

4

Metaphysics and Theology

The year 1929 was an important one for Heidegger. His old mentor, Edmund Husserl, to whom Heidegger had dedicated *Being and Time*, had retired from the chair of philosophy at the University of Freiburg, and Heidegger was recalled from Marburg to succeed him. No doubt he was happy to be back in the Black Forest region, and he made his home there for the rest of his life.

The year was important not only because of the move to Freiburg but because of some important writings which Heidegger produced at that time. Chief among them was his inaugural lecture, given when he took up his new post. It was entitled 'What is Metaphysics?'. Though quite short, this lecture is important, both as gathering up some of the issues from the unfinished *Being and Time* and as pointing forward to the later work in which the question of Being would be confronted more directly than it had been up till then.

The lecture itself is paradoxical and typically Heideggerian. It will deal with a metaphysical question. But this is not, as we might have expected, the question of Being. Rather, it is the question of nothing! *Wie steht es um das Nichts?*[1] This may be translated, 'What about nothing?' or 'How is it with the nothing?' or 'What is the status of nothing?'. But however we translate it, the question remains very odd. As Heidegger himself says, 'The question deprives itself of its own object.'[2] The very idea of 'nothing' forbids us to say that nothing is this or that or anything at all. But does that mean that there is no problem here?

Heidegger believes there is a problem, a metaphysical problem, about the nothing. Any metaphysical problem, Heidegger claims, encompasses the whole range of metaphysical problems, and also involves the questioner who raises the problem. So here we see that Heidegger is continuing the quest initiated in *Being and Time*. The question about the nothing is inseparable from the question of Being; and just as Being is an existential as well as an intellectual question for *Dasein*, so also is the question about the nothing.

This enables Heidegger to appeal in this case, as he had done in the earlier inquiry, to the disclosedness of the human situation through moods or affective states. Again, it is anxiety to which he appeals. In the mood of anxiety, we have something like an encounter with the nothing. 'In anxiety, we say, one feels "ill at ease". What is "it" that makes one feel "ill at ease"? We cannot say what "it" is . . . all things and we ourselves sink into indifference . . . We can get no hold on things. In the slipping away of beings, only this "no hold on things" comes over us and remains. Anxiety reveals the nothing.'[3] Heidegger acknowledges that this mood is rare, and many people will perhaps say they have never experienced it. Perhaps it is like a mystical experience, known only to some persons of special sensitivity, but not for that reason to be dismissed out of hand.

Heidegger tries to explain his meaning more fully. 'The nothing reveals itself in anxiety, but not as a being. Just as little is it given as an object . . . Rather, the nothing makes itself known with beings and in beings expressly as a slipping away of the whole.'[4]

So it would seem that the nothing is not just annihilation or the pure negation of Being. Indeed, it begins to look like the clearing which belongs to *Dasein* and into which beings emerge. That sense would fit the sentence, 'In the clear night of the nothing of anxiety the original openness of beings as such arises: that they are beings, and not nothing.' But in another sense, the nothing is beyond beings, almost what some of the neo-Platonists called *hyperousia*. So we read, 'Holding itself out into the nothing, *Dasein* is in every case beyond beings as a whole. This being beyond beings we call "transcendence" (*Transzendenz*).'[5] Reminding us that the word 'metaphysics' is derived from the Greek *meta ta physika*, Heidegger says, 'Metaphysics is inquiry beyond or over beings, which aims to recover them as such and as a whole for our grasp.'[6]

Heidegger also quotes a traditional axiom of metaphysics: *ex nihilo nihil fit* – from nothing, nothing comes to be. He contrasts with this the Christian doctrine of creation out of nothing, but this view is criticized on the grounds that it avoids the question of Being as such and teaches that one being, namely, God, creates all the other beings. We shall meet this criticism again in a later work, and it leads eventually to Heidegger's rejection of the metaphysical exercise, his so-called 'overcoming' of metaphysics. But at the stage reached in his inaugural lecture, he is still an enthusiast for metaphysics and even declares that it belongs to the nature of man. Science, he declares, concerns itself only with the real, or what it takes to be real, and would like 'to dismiss the nothing with a lordly wave of the hand'. But it is *Dasein*'s very nature to go beyond the beings. The lecture ended with the famous question posed by Leibniz: 'Why are there beings at all, and why not rather nothing?'⁷ This is the wonder of wonders – that there are beings, not just nothing.

There are several obscurities in this lecture, especially in the later paragraphs. Heidegger must have been aware of this, because fourteen years after the lecture was given, he wrote a Postscript, in which he tried to clear up 'misconceptions' and 'misgivings'. For instance, does the lecture (as some supposed) reinforce the nihilistic tendencies in his early thinking, or does it take us in a different direction? Then, six years after the Postscript and therefore twenty years after the original lecture, Heidegger produced an Introduction, offering further clarification. We must now look at the Postscript and Introduction, and see how they elucidate the lecture.

The original lecture was entitled 'What is Metaphysics?' and Heidegger now points out that in order to ask about metaphysics, one must have gone beyond metaphysics and must even have entered into the 'overcoming' (*Überwindung*) of metaphysics. Actually, the lecture had dealt with a specific metaphysical question: 'What is the status of nothing?'. This question raises the first of three points with which Heidegger wishes to deal. If one makes 'nothing' a leading theme for metaphysics, then must not this lead to the idea that 'everything is nothing, so that it is not worthwhile either to live or to die'?⁸ In other words, is not this an extreme form of nihilism? The second point concerns the place given to anxiety in the lecture. It has a key role in illuminating the condition of *Dasein*, according to Heidegger. But is not anxiety 'the psychic state of nervous people and cowards'? The third point considers a challenge to the intellectual status of the lecture. Logic seems to make it impossible that 'nothing' could be a theme for serious study. But logic has been disregarded in favour of an appeal to feeling and an alleged existential encounter with nothing. The lecture must therefore be 'against logic'.

Heidegger's reply on the first point is that we must get away from the idea that 'nothing' is simply the denial of everything that is: rather, this 'nothing' is literally 'no thing', it is never and nowhere another being or thing that is in addition to the things that make up the world, but is of a different order altogether from the beings. (Although he does not use the expresson here, this refers to what Heidegger was later to call the 'ontological difference', the difference between Being and beings). At one point Heidegger speaks of the nothing as 'wholly other' to beings: 'This wholly other (*schlechthin Andere*) to every being is a non-being (*Nicht-Seiende*). But this nothing has Being as its essence (*west als das Sein*).'[9] It is interesting to speculate whether at this point Heidegger owes something to Rudolf Otto, one of his colleagues at Marburg with whom he sometimes had discussions. The phrase 'wholly other' was used by Otto to designate the 'numinous', the suprarational reality which human beings experience in profound religious moments. The possibility of a connection to Otto is increased when we consider some of Heidegger's remarks about the holy later in this postscript and his use of the word 'uncanny' (*unheimlich*) in his descriptions of the mood of anxiety.[10]

Heidegger's response to the complaint that in exalting the mood of anxiety he is overvaluing a reaction which may be cowardly or even morbid is predictable, in view of all he has said about it in *Being and Time*. It needs courage to face the human situation and the threats to which it is exposed. Of course, 'anxiety' is not a particularly good translation for the German *Angst*. 'Anxiety' is perhaps too clinical a word nowadays, too reminiscent of psychiatry. Formerly the word 'dread' was used to translate *Angst*, though it may be misunderstood as just an equivalent to 'fear'. Heidegger seems eager in the Postscript to associate *Angst* with what may be called the 'higher emotions'. 'Readiness for *Angst*,' he says, 'is to say "Yes!" to the inwardness of things, to fulfill the highest demand which alone touches man to the quick. Man alone of all beings, when addressed by the voice of Being, experiences the wonder of wonders: that beings *are*.'[11] There is a religious flavour in what he says here. Close to *Angst* there dwells awe (*Scheu*) – the emotion which the human being experiences in the presence of the numinous. To quote a cryptic sentence: 'Awe clears and enfolds that region of human being within which man endures at home in the enduring.'[12]

We pass on to consider the objection that Heidegger has gone against logic in his lecture. Logic, of course, gives the rules for valid thinking. But Heidegger points out that there are many kinds of thinking, and therefore there must be a plurality of logics. We are reminded of a phrase sometimes used among British philosophers who have been influenced by the later Wittgenstein: 'Every language has its logic!' When we talk of 'logic' we usually think of the logic that is applicable to the thinking of the scientists. But this thinking is what Heidegger calls 'calculative' thinking. I doubt if he really does justice to the scientist. But at least we may concede that all thinking does not follow the same pattern. As time passed, Heidegger preferred to call himself a thinker, rather than a philosopher. He also came to believe that philosophical thinking has more in common with the thinking of the poet than it has with the thinking of the scientist. For Heidegger firmly believed that the poet, just as much as the scientist or the philosopher, is concerned to speak the truth, that is to say, to uncover Being. To quote another cryptic sentence from the Postscript, 'The thinker utters Being. The poet names the holy.'[13]

In this part of Heidegger's work, there are passages that are even more directly religious in their import. He writes of both thanksgiving and sacrifice in the human being's relation to Being. In German as in English, the words 'thinking' and 'thanking' are very similar, and Heidegger as usual exploits this verbal relationship. The thinking of Being is also a thanking. 'Original thanking', he writes, 'is the echo of Being's favour, wherein it clears a space for itself and causes the unique occurrence: that the beings are.' As regards sacrifice, he claims that 'in sacrifice there is expressed that hidden thanking which alone does homage to the grace wherewith Being has endowed the nature of man'. Sacrifice, he tells us, is at the very opposite extreme from any kind of calculation, and he offers something like a definition of sacrifice, coming very close, I think, to its essential religious significance: 'Sacrifice is taking farewell of all the beings on the way to the maintenance of the favour of Being.'[14] This language about taking farewell is, of course, directly reminiscent of the mystic, Meister Eckhart.

We have to bear in mind, however, that this Postscript to the Freiburg lecture was not written until fourteen years after the lecture was delivered, and considerable changes had taken place in Heidegger's thought during that time. If we now look at the Introduction which brings us on to 1949, the changes are even more striking. Now Heidegger comes out clearly in his disillusionment with metaphysics and his desire to achieve the 'overcoming' of metaphysics.

He begins the Introduction by quoting a passage from Descartes: 'Thus the whole of philosophy is like a tree, of which the roots are metaphysics, the trunk is physics, and the branches which come out of the trunk are the other sciences.'[15] Heidegger's project of going beyond or overcoming metaphysics is to raise a further question: What is the soil in which the roots of the tree have taken hold? What is the ground from which they receive nourishment and strength?

The ground is Being, and the inquiry into Being is a more primordial inquiry than even metaphysics. This is all made more explicit in later writings in which the ontological difference between Being and the beings is brought into the foreground. But already in the inaugural lecture and its later additions there has taken place the massive shift in primacy from *Dasein* to Being. It is not *Dasein* who invents the concept of Being, but rather Being that thinks in *Dasein*. But that point should not be pressed too far. Being and the beings seem to belong together. Father William J. Richardson has drawn attention to an important point which is easily overlooked. In the Postscript of 1943, it is said that 'Being may be without the beings, but never the beings without Being'.[16] This suggests that Being is somehow independent of beings in a way analogous to that in which God, in the teaching of St Thomas, is complete in himself apart from the creation. But Richardson noticed that when the Postscript was reprinted along with the Introduction in 1949, there had taken place an unannounced reversal of the statement about the asymmetrical relation between Being and beings. Now it was said that Being needs the beings just as the beings need Being![17]

We have seen that Heidegger ended the lecture, 'What is Metaphysics?', by quoting Leibniz's question, 'Why are there beings at all, rather than nothing?' This same question forms the opening sentence of Heidegger's book, *Introduction to Metaphysics*, so that it seems reasonable to regard this book as a sequel to 'What is Metaphysics?'. The book is based on a course of lectures given at Freiburg in 1935, revised and enlarged, and finally published in 1953.

In this book Heidegger reintroduces the question of Being. It is, he claims, the most fundamental of all questions, and he believes that everyone is grazed by this question at least once in his or her lifetime, though of course the question can take many forms and perhaps will be no more than an inarticulate wonder. Early in the book, Heidegger raises the question of how this question of Being is related to theology. To anyone who accepts the Bible as divine revelation, the question, he believes, does not arise, because the answer is already known. There are beings rather than nothing because God, the supreme being, has created these other beings. God himself has not been created: he is the self-subsistent being. But the question of Being as such is not raised at all in theology. The traditional doctrine of creation never gets beyond the beings. One being, admittedly supreme among beings, has created the others. For a person who has this faith, philosophy is, as Paul says, foolishness (I Cor. 1.20). Likewise, to the philosopher, Christian faith looks like foolishness.

Heidegger does in fact allow a genuine role for theology, but it has nothing to do with philosophy. 'There is,' he writes, 'a thinking and questioning elaboration of the world of Christian

experience, that is, of faith. That is theology.' He adds: 'Only
epochs which no longer believe in the true greatness of the task of
theology arrive at the disastrous notion that philosophy can help
to provide a refurbished theology, which will satisfy the needs
and tastes of the time.'[18] These words show that in 1935
Heidegger still held, or perhaps had returned to the understanding of theology which he found among the Protestant theologians
of Marburg in the early 1920s. That was the time of the rise of the
new theology of Bultmann, Tillich and above all Karl Barth, a
theology which explicitly rejected natural theology and was
resolved to keep philosophy at a distance and to confine itself to a
hermeneutic of faith. For such a theology, as it was at that time,
the question of Being and the ontological difference would indeed
seem the foolishness of this world.

But Heidegger fails to recognize the varieties of theology, and
the fact that it does not stand still. The theology he knew was
stuck on the level of beings, but not all theology is like that.
Tillich, for instance, whom Heidegger knew at Marburg, came
eventually to see God's relation to the creatures much in the same
terms as Heidegger visualized the relation of Being to beings.
According to Tillich, God is not a being, not even the supreme
being, but Being itself. Tillich was not the first to say something
like that. Some theologians had been teaching such a doctrine of
God at least from the time of Dionysius the Areopagite, who
spoke of God as *hyperousia*, 'beyond being'. Even writers who
stood nearer to the tradition of biblical theism, including
St Thomas, though they used the term *ens*, 'a being', in referring
to God, qualified the word *ens* in such ways as to indicate that this
is not another *ens* in addition to all the innerworldly *entia*, but a
quite unique reality who might even be considered 'wholly other'
to finite entities.

Heidegger lumps together all theologies under the blanket
expression, 'onto-theology',[19] but he cannot be allowed to decide
what is to count as theology. In spite of his early interest in
theology, the time came when he felt it necessary to write:
'Someone who has experienced theology in his own roots, both
the theology of the Christian faith and that of philosophy, would
today rather remain silent about God when he is speaking in the

realm of thinking.'[20] This is a perfectly reasonable attitude to take, but it does not qualify the one who takes it to make sweeping pronouncements about theology. I have already suggested that scientists too are treated somewhat cavalierly by Heidegger, and we shall see further evidence that the thinking of theologians and scientists alike is given less than its due.

We can only say that, apart from his early enthusiasm for Catholic thought, Heidegger had a strangely ambiguous attitude toward theology, what might properly be called a 'love-hate' relationship. Theological questions obviously fascinated him, and he touches on them rather frequently. Yet he interpreted his vocation as a philosopher or thinker as demanding that he must steer clear of any theological involvement, and this was his position during the greater part of his career. In 1927, the year when *Being and Time* was published, he gave a lecture on 'Phenomenology and Theology', and the policy which he sketched out at that time was one to which he continued to adhere. The main points of that policy were: (1) theology is founded on faith and concerns itself with the hermeneutics of faith; (2) faith, in turn, is a historical mode of being; (3) theology is therefore through and through a historical science; (4) as such, theology belongs to the positive sciences, that is to say, it deals with a specific region of human experience (the Christian revelation), and is therefore unlike the generalizing scope of philosophy, especially when the latter is understood as the quest for the meaning of Being as such.

Incidentally, this early lecture of Heidegger on theology lay unpublished for about forty years. But it seems likely that the standoffish attitude which it expresses remained, however much Heidegger's thinking may have changed during these forty years. Even those who are eager to enrol Heidegger among the theologians recognize his unwillingness to accept any theological commitment. Thus, although we have noted that Gadamer regarded Heidegger as a spokesman for Christianity rather than for secularism, we find him also wondering why someone who had been as deeply stirred by theological questions as he thought Heidegger had been, did not himself become a theologian but deliberately sought to distance himself from theology. 'Because', says Gadamer, 'he was a thinker, it was thinking that was at work in him. He felt no empowerment to speak of God. But what would be needed to speak of God, and that it would not do to speak of him as the sciences speak of their objects, that was the question that stirred him and showed him the path of thinking.'[21] All of which may be perfectly true, but it seems to imply that theology and thinking are entirely different enterprises!

But now we must come back to Heidegger's *Introduction to Metaphysics*, for so far we have considered only Heidegger's distinction of the question of Being from any theological or metaphysical doctrine of creation. Actually, the remainder of the book consists largely of repetitions or elucidations of points that Heidegger has made elsewhere in his writings. We can note only some of the more striking passages in the book.

Perhaps the most striking of all is Heidegger's interpretation of a chorus from Sophocles' drama, *Antigone*. It begins:

There is much that is strange, but nothing
That surpasses man in strangeness.

The word here translated 'strange' is *deinos*, a very strong word which has connotations of awe and terror. The whole passage readily lends itself to a Heideggerian interpretation. The human being, the *Dasein*, is the strangest of all, but the world in which he lives is pervaded by the strange. As we might expect, Heidegger equates the *deinos* with the uncanny (*unheimlich*) and, as was already suggested, the word 'numinous' might not be inappropriate. Sophocles depicts the human race struggling to overcome nature and subdue the earth, but the adventure ends inevitably with death. Heidegger is at pains to deny that the struggle is to be interpreted in any evolutionary way. In line with his doctrine of truth as the moment of uncovering or revelation, the great moment is the beginning. The chorus is not 'a narrative of man's development from the savage hunter and primitive sailor to the civilized builder of cities. The basic fallacy underlying such modes of thought consists in the belief that history begins with the primitive and the backward, the weak and helpless. The opposite is true. The beginning is the strangest and mightiest. What comes afterward is not development but the flattening that results from mere spreading out; it is inability to retain the beginning.'[22]

There are at least three points to be noted in connection with Heidegger's quotation from Sophocles. The first has already come to our attention. It is the idea that human beings become human, lay hold on an authentic humanity, not through a long and gradual process but from some overwhelming moment of vision, some revelation of Being bursting upon them and then, perhaps, gradually fading. The second point is that although Heidegger would acknowledge that the Christian revelation was one such moment of vision and is the proper subject for theological study, he himself seems to look to ancient Greece for the decisive vision. So when we find him making statements that appear to have a religious import, we must not be too quick in giving them a Christian interpretation, for Heidegger, as has indeed become apparent in what we have learned from his *Introduction to Metaphysics*, seems to find more inspiration in Sophocles, Parmenides and Heraclitus than in the Bible. The third point is that his use of Sophocles' chorus illustrates his belief that perhaps it is the poet rather than the scientist or the theologian who can best help the thinker in his quest for the meaning of Being.

Other topics raised in the book we are presently considering are being and becoming, being and appearing, being and thinking and being and the 'ought'. The first three of these relationships we already considered in connection with Heidegger's attempted reconciliation of the ideas of Parmenides and Heraclitus.[23] The fourth topic, Being and the 'ought' or Being and obligation, is one that we would very much like to hear about, for it seems to promise an ethical dimension to Heidegger's philosophy. Yet he devotes to it only a couple of pages that do not seem to say very much. But he does tell us that 'to forget Being and cultivate only the beings – that is nihilism'.[24]

There is one other work from this period of Heidegger's philosophical activity which seems to me to bring together the new ideas which he worked out after 1929. This work, which is quite brief (less than fifty pages) is called in German *Über den Humanismus*, and in English is usually called *A Letter on*

Humanism. It dates from 1947, and originated as a letter to the French philosopher, Jean Beaufret. It is important as marking Heidegger's definitive dissociation of his teaching from the 'existentialism' of Sartre, and the mention of humanism is presumably an allusion to Sartre's 'Existentialism is a Humanism'.

Early in the letter, we find evidence of Heidegger's admiration for the originality of the Greeks. His French friends are asking him about the viability of humanism. But do we need words like 'humanism'? 'Such names begin to flourish only when original thinking comes to an end. During the time of their greatness, the Greeks thought without such headings. They did not even call thinking "philosophy".'[25]

Presumably with the saying of Parmenides in mind, Heidegger tells us that 'thinking is the thinking of Being. The genitive says something twofold. Thinking is of Being inasmuch as thinking, coming from Being, belongs to Being. At the same time, thinking is of Being insofar as thinking, belonging to Being, listens to Being.'[26] This implies the primacy of Being over the beings and over *Dasein*, and this is made explicit: Being itself 'presides over thinking and hence over the essence of humanity, and that means over its relation to Being'.[27] What Heidegger is saying here is also an attack on the metaphysics of subjectivity, the belief that the human mind is the measure of everything. To get away from any hint of subjectivism, Heidegger writes in this essay 'ek-sistence' rather than 'existence', stressing that it denotes a 'standing out into the truth of Being'. He contrasts this position with the view of Sartre who 'stays with metaphysics in oblivion of the truth of Being'.[28]

The decisive point in this clash between Heidegger and Sartre is reached when Heidegger claims that Sartre has misread a sentence in *Being and Time*. There we read: 'Only as long as *Dasein* is (that is, only as long as an understanding of Being is ontically possible), "is there" Being.'[29] At first sight this seems to confirm Sartre's belief that human subjectivity is the ultimate, that human thinking has produced 'Being' as its own creation, that '*précisement nous sommes sur un plan où il y a seulement des hommes.*'[30] But Heidegger points out that there are inverted commas round the words translated 'there is' to draw attention to the fact that in German the expression is *es gibt*, literally, 'it gives', though often used idiomatically in the weak sense of 'there is'. Here it is to be taken in the literal sense, 'it gives Being'. So we ask, who or what gives Being? The answer is that Being gives itself. 'The "it" that here "gives" is Being itself. The "gives" names the essence of Being that is giving or granting its truth. The self-giving into the open, along with the open region itself, is Being itself.'[31] So, Heidegger tells us, Sartre's sentence should read, *'précisement nous sommes sur un plan où il y a principalement l'Être.'* So where does that take us?

Heidegger does explicitly dissociate himself from Sartre's atheism, and also from humanism, if that is taken to mean that man is on his own in the universe, or is master of the universe. He does not, of course, reject humanism in the sense of respect for human beings and human personality. But although Being has been described here as a self-giving, and in other parts of the essay is accorded qualities that have been traditionally given to God, Heidegger tells us that Being is not the same as God and that his own philosophy is neither theistic nor atheistic. We shall have to ask later what this might mean. But for the present two points seem to have been established – the first is that Being is not the product of man or *Dasein*, and the second that 'man is not the lord of the beings, but the shepherd of Being.'[32]

Did Heidegger really understand things in this way when he wrote *Being and Time*? Or was it only twenty years later, when challenged by Sartre and having pondered things more deeply, that he arrived at this interpretation? We cannot know the answer to that question, but he does point out that if we go back to *Being and Time*, we shall find there the assertion that Being is the 'absolute *transcendens*'. But it is not altogether clear what this expression means. If theism is defined in terms that demand a personal God, then perhaps the *transcendens* cannot be deemed theistic, because it is conceived as impersonal or suprapersonal. But at least the question of theism remains open.

Quoting from another of his writings, *Vom Wesen des Grundes*, Heidegger says: 'Through the ontological interpretation of *Dasein* as being-in-the-world, no decision, whether affirmative or negative, is made concerning a possible being toward God. It is, however, the case that through an illumination of transcendence we first achieve an *adequate concept of Dasein*, with respect to which it can now be asked how the relationship of *Dasein* to God is ontologically ordered.' In the next paragraph, he offers the following series of steps in the quest for God. 'Only from the truth of Being can the essence of the holy be thought. Only from the essence of the holy is the essence of divinity to be thought. Only in the light of the essence of divinity can it be thought or said what the word "God" is to signify.' It would seem that at this point Heidegger is acknowledging that, after all, there is common ground between philosophy and theology.

I attach particular importance to Heidegger's cutting down of the human being to proper size, by denying that he is the master of the world or the measure of all things; and likewise I attach importance to the assertion that the essence of Being itself is self-giving. Both of these seem to be highly compatible with Christianity.

Toward the end of the essay, Heidegger comments on that story of Heraclitus to which I alluded in chapter 1, which tells how some strangers came to visit the philosopher, and were astonished by the meanness of his dwelling, and even more astonished when they went in and found him shivering beside a stove. He invited them in, saying, 'Even the gods present themselves here!' Heidegger comments: 'The group of visitors, in their importunate curiosity about the thinker, are disappointed and perplexed by their first glimpse of his abode. They believe that they should meet the thinker in circumstances which, contrary to the ordinary round of human life, everywhere bear traces of the exceptional and rare and so of the exciting. The group hope that in their visit to the thinker they will find things that will provide material for entertaining conversation – at least for a while. The strangers expect to catch sight of the thinker perchance at that very moment when, sunk in profound meditation, he is thinking. They want this experience not in order to be overwhelmed by thinking, but simply so they can say they saw and heard someone everybody says is a thinker. Instead of this, the sightseers find Heraclitus by a stove. That is surely a common and insignificant place. True enough, bread is baked there. But Heraclitus is not even baking. He stands there merely to warm himself. In this altogether everyday place he betrays the whole poverty of his life. Yet even here the gods present themselves.'[33] Is there some parallel between this picture and that of a man dying on a cross and so making present the very life of God?

5

Thinghood, Technology, Art

In this chapter and in the one which follows, I intend to fill out this account of Heidegger's thought by dealing with various topics which have either not yet come to our notice or have been treated only briefly or as they found expression in his early writings. We have already seen that, beginning from the inaugural lecture, 'What is Metaphysics?' and the additions that were made to it, Heidegger was moving away from the apparently atheistic and narrowly humanistic or even Promethean beliefs which some interpreters, notably Sartre, had read into *Being and Time*. By the time we get to the *Letter on Humanism*, which belongs to the year 1947, we seem to be in a very different world, though Heidegger himself tended to minimize the extent of the 'turning' (*Kehre*) that had taken place in his thought and interpreted the new or apparently new ideas as developments of what was already implicit in the early writings. But, of course, even he plainly admitted that the path which he had first tried to follow had broken off, and this fact is amply attested by the unfinished state of *Being and Time*.

The first topic to be considered is Heidegger's answer to the question, 'What is a thing?' and the way he was answering this question in the 1950s was decidedly different from what he was saying in 1927 in *Being and Time*.[1] Heidegger is still maintaining that a thing is not primarily a material object 'present-at-hand' for our observation. That objective view of a thing is derivative from a much more intimate relation to the thing. The tendency in Western thought has been to think of the world as a collection of things set over against us, and of *Dasein* itself, not indeed as another thing, but as another entity 'present-at-hand'. But *Dasein* is not just another item in the world, not even another rather special item, to be designated by the word 'person'. *Dasein* is certainly 'Being-in-the-world' and there can be no worldless *Dasein*, but *Dasein*'s Being-in-the-world is quite different from the 'innerworldly' (*innerweltlich*) being that belongs to things. *Dasein* transcends the world, and gives to the world its unity as world, for *Dasein* is the point from which the world is seen and understood. The multitude of things contained in the world are seen and understood in the context of world, within which they are connected in a network with each other and with *Dasein*.[2]

These things are seen by *Dasein* as not just present-at-hand or lying about, but as ready-to-hand, available for use by *Dasein* in its concernful dealings with the world. For *Dasein*'s Being-in-the-world is not that of an observer, but of one who 'dwells' in the world, one who has to carve out a living in the world. Thus the things of the world become for *Dasein* equipment (*Zeug*) for living. As Heidegger reminded us,[3] the Greek word for 'thing' was *pragma*, something that we employ in our *praxeis*, 'activities'. For *Dasein*, the things of the world become increasingly a closely knit system of instruments that are serviceable to *Dasein*. This is true not only of artefacts, but even of natural objects which are incorporated into the instrumental system. Today, even a wilderness area may be designated a 'national park' and it becomes, so to speak, equipment for recreation. Thus the world is more and more a human project.

The example of a thing which Heidegger chooses to illustrate his theory is a hammer. If we ask, 'What is a hammer?' the question is not answered by an objective description of the hammer as an object in isolation as merely one of the many things within the world. It can, of course, be described in that way – we might be told that the head of the hammer is iron, that the shaft is such-and-such a kind of wood, and so on, but we would not have begun to understand a hammer. We understand it only when we see someone hammering, and then we understand also its relations to nails and to wood and to such human activities as building and furnishing – in other words, we understand it in the context of a world. The world is already implied in the hammer, for the world, like *Dasein*, is not another thing, but an *a priori* conception which enables us to see things in their being, that is, for what they are. We see the hammer as a piece of equipment for hammering, we see the automobile as a piece of equipment for transport, and so on.

Now, this whole way of looking at the world may seem very utilitarian and down-to-earth, and indeed it is, for in the division of *Being and Time* in which he discusses the world, Heidegger does say that he is confining his analysis to 'everyday' existence and he even speaks of the world as a workshop.[4] But the way remains open to a fuller or richer understanding of the world and this does in fact come, though not explicitly until about twenty years later.

The new understanding comes in an essay called 'The Thing' ('*Das Ding*')[5] of the year 1950, though we already note a preliminary allusion to it in the little piece about 'The Country Lane', written in 1949 and discussed in chapter 1.[6] It is an understanding which gets away from the somewhat exploitative attitude to the world expounded in *Being and Time* and accords more with the claim in the *Letter on Humanism* that 'man is not the lord of beings, but the shepherd of Being'.[7]

The new view is expressed in terms of what Heidegger calls the 'fourfold' or the 'quadrate'[8] (*das Geviert*). A thing is not only more than an object, it is more even than a human product or an item in the human equipment for bringing the earth under control. A thing is now granted the possibility of having a beauty and dignity of its own. What then is this 'fourfold' or 'quadrate'? It means that everything has a fourfold reference, or has four dimensions of being which together constitute the meaning of that thing. The four dimensions are: earth and sky, mortals and gods. On hearing these words, we may wonder whether Heidegger has not slipped over from philosophy into the realm of myth or poetry. Perhaps he has, but this would not trouble him very much. Even in *Being and Time*, he introduced a classical myth about Care into the middle of his existential analytic, on the ground that this myth shows us a pre-scientific understanding of *Dasein* which anticipates the results of phenomenological analysis; and likewise, from early in his career, he had recognized that poetry is by no means merely an emotive or non-cognitive type of utterance, but a way to truth, even truth at the deepest level, so that the thinker may find that he has more in common with the poet than with the scientist.

Just as he had used the example of a hammer to illustrate his early understanding of the nature of a thing, Heidegger now chooses the example of a wine-jug or pitcher to elucidate what he means by the fourfold. The jug refers to earth, because the material of which it is made, some kind of clay, has been taken out of the earth. It refers to the sky, from which has come both sunshine and rain to swell and ripen the grapes used for making wine. Then there is the human reference – the jug is the work of a skilled craftsman or artist, the potter who has given to it the form of a wine-jug. And what about the gods? The wine-jug may be used for pouring a libation. Just as with the hammer, it was the act of hammering which revealed the being of the hammer, so with the jug, it is the act of pouring out the wine that shows us what the jug *is*.

Admittedly, one may feel that Heidegger has to strain matters a little in order to make the fourfold fit the jug, or possibly to make the jug fit the fourfold schema. It is the act of pouring that is said to show us the jug as it is, and presumably, that means in its unity, for we are told that the four aspects of the jug all belong together and each implies the others. But can we achieve greater clarity about this 'fourfold'?

Although I said that the language of Heidegger about the fourfold seems to be poetic rather than strictly philosophical, his use of the scheme can hardly fail to remind us of Aristotle's doctrine of the four causes.[9] According to Aristotle, every thing has a material cause – his example is the bronze out of which a statue is made, and we can see that this corresponds to the clay of the wine-jug. Then there is the formal cause. The statue is, let us say, a statue of Apollo and the bronze has been cast into the form which the artist visualized as that of the god. It is not so easy to see how this could correspond to the sky, in Heidegger's scheme. Third comes the activity which has produced the statue, namely, the work of the artist and his assistants. This third type of cause is often called the 'efficient' cause, but Heidegger himself, in a brief discussion of the Aristotelian causes, points out that Aristotle does not use any adjective that might be translated as 'efficient'.

While it may have been natural for the Greeks to think of a person as the 'cause' of a statue, such language would be very odd in English. The Greek word which we translate 'cause' (*aitia*) had a different semantic range, being more personal and connected with the notion of responsibility, while the English word is normally used of impersonal causation. We might think it was somewhat degrading to describe a human being as a 'cause', and certainly Heidegger held that it was degrading to God to describe him as 'first cause'. We can, however, recognize a broad correspondence between Heidegger's recognition of the mortal or human aspect of a thing and the kind of agency covered by Aristotle's third type of cause. The fourth item in Heidegger's fourfold, the gods, is once more difficult to relate to Aristotle's final cause – something is done or made 'for the sake of' something or someone. If the being of the wine-jug is revealed not just in pouring wine but specifically in pouring a libation, then perhaps we could say that in Heidegger the end (*telos*) of the artefact is to glorify the gods. We might in turn link this with what Heidegger has said about sacrifice in the Postscript to 'What is Metaphysics?'[10]

There are, of course, other questions that may be raised at this point. What, for instance, does Heidegger mean by 'the gods'? Probably he uses this expression because of his fascination with the Greeks, and likewise with the poetry of Hölderlin, in which there are many mentions of the gods. It would be wrong to read into the expression 'God' in a theistic sense, but the word 'gods' does stand for what might be called a 'divine factor' in all reality, something holy in which every thing participates. The early Heidegger seemed to be depicting a world that is entirely secular and governed by utilitarian considerations. Heidegger has not drawn back from his view that temporality and historicity belong to all reality, not just humanity but also Being and the gods. But in the philosophy that he develops in his middle years, he finds room within time and history for the divine and for the human spirit with its aspirations. As I have remarked before, this is not a Christian philosophy, perhaps there is no such thing as a Christian philosophy, but it is compatible with Christianity, and that no doubt explains its attraction for some of the leading theologians of the twentieth century.

But how does this highly idiosyncratic theory of the thing as fourfold apply in the technological society in which we nowadays live? One can see that the early Heidegger's way of seeing the world in terms of the ready-to-hand as a kind of vast workshop would be a philosophy almost tailor-made for the technological world, but in broadening his conception of thinghood, he seems to have moved over to some form of romanticism. This might be understandable, when we remember that Heidegger is a man of the countryside. Yet on the other hand it would be hard to square with those important elements in his thought which reflect the spirit of the twentieth century. Is there a split in Heidegger's thinking? Is he trying to come to terms with the actual world that we know and inhabit today, while at the same time clinging to past ideas that are just not able to find a secure place in our current ways of thinking?

These problems emerge very acutely if we consider what Heidegger says about technology, and I doubt if clear answers are to be had. He has in fact been very much aware of the dominating role that technology has come to play in the contemporary world, but what he has written on the subject[11] is both obscure and ambiguous, and the confusion seems to have spread to his commentators. On the one hand, Heidegger obviously cannot be happy with technology, because it seems to commit what for him is the cardinal sin of becoming absorbed in the beings and so becoming oblivious of Being; yet on the other hand, common sense tells him that we are *already* (a fateful word in Heidegger!) up to our necks in technology and there is no way back, so we have to learn to live with it. As with so many other matters in both public and private life, it is too late to ask whether we want to live in a technological society, for such a society is already our factical situation.

I complained that Heidegger's treatment of technology is obscure. He tells us that the essence of technology is 'enframing' (*Ge-stell*) and this in turn is described as a 'gathering together' in which the world is regarded as a kind of fund of goods, or a stock of goods for production and consumption. The motivation behind this vast activity is the will to power. But the trouble, as Heidegger sees it, is that the said vast activity seems to have no clearcut goals. This is expressed quite clearly in one of his essays where he writes about the harnessing of the Rhine for the production of electric power. 'The hydroelectric plant is set into the current of the Rhine. It sets the Rhine to supplying its hydraulic pressure, which then sets the turbines turning. This turning sets those machines in motion whose thrust sets going the electric current: the energy concealed in nature is unlocked, what is unlocked is transformed, what is transformed is stored up, what is stored up is distributed, and what is distributed is switched about ever anew.'[12] Perhaps these sentences help to clarify in a concrete way what is meant by the abstract term *Ge-stell*. Clearly, however, there is a touch of irony or even of caricature in Heidegger's word picture, a hastening on from one phase of activity to the next, without much idea of the final destination. There is also something like nostalgia in Heidegger's final remark: 'Even the Rhine itself appears as something at our command.' The great river has been reduced to a piece of equipment. I imagine that the Rhine is to the Germans like the Volga to the Russians or the Nile to the Egyptians, not just a fourfold but a manifold, with innumerable links to the nation, its history and its mythology.

Ambiguous too is the way in which technology has gained its hold upon humanity. We have noted Heidegger's acknowledgment that it is too late for people to wonder whether or not they wish to live in a technological society. They are already in it, and have to make the best of it. But how did they get into it? Was that the result of some initial decisions in the past? Heidegger seems to suggest that the technological era is a destiny which Being sends on the human race.[13] 'Enframing sends into a way of revealing. Enframing is an ordaining of destiny, as is every revealing.' We have already met this notion of destiny in Heidegger, and I think we should feel uneasy about it. But after saying that 'destining holds complete sway over men', Heidegger suddenly changes course, and tells us: 'That destining is never a fate that compels. For man becomes truly free only in so far as he belongs to the realm of destining and so becomes one who listens, though not one who simply obeys.'[14]

Can we disentangle some reasonably clear teaching about technology from the obscurities, ambiguities and paradoxes which Heidegger has employed in expounding his ideas on the subject? I shall try, but I do not venture to claim that what I say represents what Heidegger thought, or that other interpreters would agree with my findings.

A point from which we may begin and which is, I think, indisputable, is Heidegger's contention that whether we like it or not, we have come into a technological age. We need not, of course, accept Heidegger's further claim that this is some kind of destiny (*Geschick*) that Being has sent upon us. We may have got into it by the choices made by our ancestors, but however it may have come about, it is part, even the dominant part, of our factical heritage, so that we have to come to terms with it and live as members of a technological society.

I think we can further agree with Heidegger that there is a danger in technology. The danger is that what was originally instrument and equipment runs out of control and begins to determine the lives of those who were its masters. I suppose we were chiefly conscious of this at the time when the arms race between East and West was at its height, when deadly weapons were being piled up in that stock or store which is typical of *Gestell*, and when we all seemed helpless to prevent a race to destruction. That particular danger has receded, but the general danger remains that humanity itself becomes part of the stock.

One further point in Heidegger's analysis seems to me acceptable, namely, his belief that the cure for the dangers of technology cannot come from technology itself. When something goes wrong in some part of the system, the temptation is to believe that an improved technology will put it right. But that could be the case only within narrow limits. Technology, as Heidegger indicates in his remarks on the use of the Rhine, is instrumental, or, at least, if it has goals, these are either ill-defined or short-term. We need more clarity about goals, but these are not fixed by technology. At this point, however, we might blame Heidegger himself for never having developed an ethical side to his philosophy. Indeed, it could be complained with some justice that from his early thinking onward, he consistently avoided ethical questions.

In the last part of his essay on 'The Question Concerning Technology', Heidegger seems to raise our hopes, but even there the ethical question is passed by. He writes, 'The threat to man does not come in the first instance from the potentially lethal machines and apparatus of technology. The actual threat has already affected man in his essence. The rule of enframing (*Gestell*) threatens man with the possibility that it could be denied to him to enter into a more original revealing and hence to experience the call of a more primal truth. Thus, when enframing reigns, there is *danger* in the highest sense.' But he quotes Hölderlin:

> But where danger is, grows
>> The saving power also.

The very danger of technology pushes toward a new revealing. Heidegger reminds us that in ancient Greece *techne* was the word used for both craft and art. Perhaps in the fine arts we may find a way forward, and it is to art that we turn in the third and final part of this chapter.

Heidegger's views on art, especially visual art, are to be found chiefly in a lengthy essay, 'The Origin of the Work of Art' (*Der Ursprung des Kunstwerkes*), published in 1950.[15] It had originated in a lecture as early as 1935, but this lecture was later revised and expanded to become a series of three lectures. Towards the end of the lecture, he claims that it is 'the linguistic work [of art], namely, poetry, that has a privileged place among the arts',[16] and he wrote quite a few pieces on poetry, especially the poetry of Hölderlin. But we shall leave consideration of poetry until later, and for the present confine ourselves to 'The Origin of the Work of Art', where his concern is mainly with such arts as architecture and painting.

Most people, Heidegger thinks, would find the origin of the work of art in the artist. We think of him or her as the one who creates the work. But this answer is not satisfactory, for we may then want to ask, why do we call this person an artist? Is it not the case that the artist becomes an artist and is recognized as an artist with the production of the work of art? 'The artist is the origin of the work. The work is the origin of the artist. Neither is without the other . . . In themselves and in their interrelations, artist and work *are* each of them by virtue of a third thing which is prior to both, namely, that which also gives artist and work of art their names – art.'[17] So there is a circularity in naming the artist as the origin of the work, and we have to search more deeply.

The work is itself a thing. Indeed, in the modern world where art like sport and virtually everything else have become commercialized, works of art are shipped around from one exhibition to another and from one auction room to another 'like coal from the Ruhr and logs from the Black Forest', as Heidegger expresses it. Works of art are undoubtedly things. But can anything about art be derived from this fact of thingliness?

In the context of this essay, Heidegger raises the question which he has already raised in *Being and Time* and will raise again in other essays, 'What is a thing?'. It was just about the time when 'The Origin of the Work of Art' was published that Heidegger was working on his idea of the 'fourfold' as constituting the nature of thinghood.[18] The fourfold does not appear explicitly even in the final version of 'The Origin', though we shall see that something rather like it was in his mind. But when he first discusses the nature of a thing in this essay, he is criticizing views which he had already criticized in *Being and Time* – views in which a thing is considered primarily in objective terms as something which confronts *Dasein* in an external way as an item encountered in the environment. We need not go into these criticisms in detail, because in principle they add nothing to what he had said earlier. It brings us round to the equipmental view of the thing developed in *Being and Time*, where the thing is viewed pragmatically as belonging with a world projected by *Dasein*.

At this point, Heidegger introduces an example, and as usual the concrete illustration goes far to clarify some of his more abstract utterances. The example of a thing which he chooses is a pair of peasant shoes. Such a pair of shoes is thingly, but we are reminded that it can also be a theme for art. There is a famous painting by Vincent Van Gogh of a pair of peasant shoes, and this painting is skilfully used by Heidegger to link thinghood with art. I suppose that peasant shoes would not usually be considered in themselves a work of art. They are certainly equipment, and like the other equipment we have considered, are understood when we see them in use – when the owner of the shoes is wearing them at work in the fields. But they would seem to be objects of utility rather than of beauty. But how then was Van Gogh able to make them the subject of his painting? Perhaps the answer is that although a ready-to-hand thing is characterized by utility rather than beauty, some element of beauty may be there. Shoes specially made for, let us say, a princess or a ballerina might be a work of art as well as a piece of equipment. Heidegger does suggest that it would be hard to draw a hard-and-fast line of demarcation between the craftsman and the artist, both of whom are designated in Greek by the same word, *technites*. Perhaps there is no well-formed piece of equipment that does not begin to have the properties of a work of art; while, on the other hand, the good artist who works in stone or metal or pigment will be also a craftsman.

There is a remarkable paragraph in which Heidegger talks about the significance of the peasant shoes in the Van Gogh picture: 'From the dark opening of the worn insides of the shoes the toilsome tread of the worker stares forth. In the stiffly rugged heaviness of the shoes there is the accumulated tenacity of her slow trudge through the far-spreading and ever-uniform furrows of the field swept by a raw wind . . . This equipment is pervaded by uncomplaining worry as to the certainty of bread, the wordless joy of having once more withstood want, the trembling before the impending childbed and shivering at the surrounding menace of death.'[19] I have curtailed this passage severely, but we see how the work of art draws out into the open, shall we say, the manifold reference of the thing which it portrays – whether a fourfold reference or even something more to a sensitive imagination. Heidegger specifically mentions that the equipment belongs to the *earth* (the first item in the fourfold) and then that it belongs also to the *world* of the peasant woman, and perhaps that world embraces the remaining three items.

But, he adds, perhaps it is only in the picture that we notice all this about the shoes. Perhaps a pair of shoes by themselves would not call forth such reflections. What about the woman who wears them? Does she not simply wear them? Heidegger thinks there is more to her experience than that. She presumably does not reflect on the shoes in the manner that Heidegger did on seeing them in Van Gogh's picture, but she believes in the reliability of her equipment and this amounts to being implicitly sure of her world.

What then happens when we are confronted with Van Gogh's painting? As Heidegger expresses it, the painting *speaks*. 'It discloses what the equipment *is* in truth.' For the Greeks, as we have heard often enough from Heidegger, truth is the unconcealedness of beings. 'If there occurs in the work [of art] a disclosure of a particular being, disclosing what and how it is, then there is here an occurring, a happening of truth at work. In the work of art, the truth of beings has set itself to work . . . Some particular being, a pair of peasant shoes, comes in the work to stand in the light of its Being. The Being of beings comes into the steadiness of its shining.'[20] Heidegger seems to be suggesting here that the discovery of truth is not just the result of a human search, but that Being opens itself in truth. The Greek word *physis*, usually translated as 'nature', would, according to Heidegger, be better translated as 'emergence.' Furthermore, *physis* is 'being' and is cognate with the English word. So we could say 'Being is emergence'. If one accepts this, then art, which, it was argued, is prior both to the artist and to the work of art, has its origin in Being. 'The essence of art would then be this: the truth of beings setting itself to work.'[21] Heidegger goes so far as to say that in great art, the artist remains inconsequential compared with the work. Could we say of the work of art that it brings into the open, into unconcealedness, what was already there implicitly in the beings represented in the art-work? If everything is fourfold in its nature, then is its character unfolded in the work of art? This might sometimes be the case, and it might be an acceptable interpretation of Van Gogh's picture of the pair of shoes. But art comes in so many guises that the interpretation would sometimes fail.

Heidegger soon brings forward another illustration, also taken from the visual arts, but this time from architecture, and unlike Van Gogh's picture, the architectural work of art does not represent any thing. The example is a Greek temple. It stands in a valley, and enclosed within it is the figure of the god, concealed yet hallowing the whole precinct. This temple gathers around itself not just a fourfold but a manifold field of meaning in which there is the unity of 'those paths and relations in which birth and death, disaster and blessing, victory and disgrace, endurance and decline acquire the shape of destiny for human being'.[22]

Heidegger is not normally an elegant writer, but occasionally he does rise to a considerable height of eloquence. He did that when he wrote about the peasant woman's shoes in Van Gogh's picture, and he does it again when he writes about the temple: 'Standing there, the building rests on the rocky ground. This resting of the work draws up out of the rock the obscurity of that rock's bulky but spontaneous support. Standing there, the building holds its own against the storm raging above it and so first makes the storm itself manifest in its violence. The lustre and gleam of the stone, though itself apparently glowing only by the grace of the sun, yet first brings to radiance the light of the day, the breadth of the sky, the darkness of the night. The temple's firm towering makes visible the invisible spaces of air. The steadfastness of the work contrasts with the surge of the surf, and its own repose brings out the raging of the sea.'[23] This emerging and rising in itself illustrates what was meant by *physis*, and likewise it illustrates the meaning of stable earth.

Heidegger comes near at this point to a sacramental view of the universe. As long as the figure of the god remains in the temple and offerings are made, the sense of the holy is there. The statue is not just a portrait of the god, to make it easier for us to imagine him. It is a work [of art] that lets the god be present, and thus *is* the god himself.

But the important words in Heidegger's discussion are the contrasted terms, 'earth' and 'world'. The work of art sets up a world and it sets forth the earth. This setting (*stellen*) is obviously very different from the setting we met in *Ge-stell*, the 'enframing' that is typical of technology. Neither is it some imaginary framework that we subjectively add to the multitude of things we encounter in the world. The world, as we have already learned, is not a mere collection of things. 'The *world worlds*, and is more fully in being than the tangible and perceptible realm in which we believe ourselves to be at home.'[24]

World and earth contrast with each other, are even at strife with each other because, in the setting up of a world, things are brought into the light of being and truth, things that have long been concealed in the depth of earth. A simple example which symbolizes the whole process is the bringing forth of the marble for the temple from under the earth. For the first time, it can be marble in all the beauty of polished gleaming stone. This illustrates another point which Heidegger makes, and although he was writing long before the environmental question became a burning issue, what he said still has relevance. When the earth's material is used equipmentally, it is at the same time *used up*; art, on the other hand, lets things be what they really are.

Yet world and earth are not just to be contrasted, they need each other. As Heidegger says more than once, earth juts into the world. Although he does not himself use the illustration, his words remind me of the Dome of the Rock at Jerusalem, where through the smooth floor of the sanctuary there juts forth the rocky peak of Mount Moriah on which the building has been erected. According to tradition, it was there that Abraham was about to sacrifice Isaac, many centuries before there was any temple or mosque on the spot.

The concept of 'world' which we find in these middle and later writings of Heidegger has developed far from that instrumental world of work which he expounded in *Being and Time*. Whether it incorporates that fourfold conception of the thing which Heidegger uses in some of his writings is a matter for debate. It certainly moves toward a much richer conception than is found in the early writings, but perhaps the fourfold was spelled out too precisely, and certainly there is difficulty in applying it to particular cases. The simpler or seemingly simpler conception of earth and world is also more flexible. But whatever of these two conceptions we prefer, I think both do justice to the richness of human experience, and to the being of *Dasein* who exists simultaneously in truth and untruth.

6

Thinking, Language, Poetry

In this chapter, as in the one which precedes it, we shall direct our attention to three topics that were important for Heidegger and that are closely related to one another – thinking, language and poetry. In seeking to understand the progression of his thought on these topics, we shall pay special attention to those moments in his thinking which touch closely on the questions which are the main concern of this book, Heidegger's relation to Christianity and how this is influenced by his understanding of time and temporality.

In the early writings, there is not much explicit discussion about thinking in general. We have, however, already noted that Heidegger had quite a lot to say about phenomenology and that he adopted its methods in order to carry out the existential analytic in *Being and Time*.[1] Phenomenology is a way of thinking, a way which is strict and disciplined, and which was claimed by Husserl and his followers to be 'scientific' (*wissenschaftlich*) in the broad sense in which that word is understood among German academics. A major characteristic of phenomenology is the emphasis which it lays upon *description* as distinct from inference and speculation. This was the type of thinking that Heidegger employed in setting forth the ontology of *Dasein*. As William Richardson expresses it, 'If phenomenology is the method chosen for the meditation upon *Dasein* which is to prepare the way to interrogate the sense of Being itself, this means that it is the way that the Heidegger of 1927 goes about the *thinking of Being*.'[2] We ought to note the use of the word 'meditation' in Richardson's remark. 'Meditation' suggests a kind of thought in which the mind is docile and receptive to whatever it is thinking about. Such thought may be contrasted

with the active investigative thought of the natural sciences as
they probe into the properties and behaviour of the various
domains of nature. It would be going too far to say that
Heidegger is against science, but it cannot be denied that on more
than one occasion, he bluntly declares that science does not
think![3] To hear that science does not think is a surprise to those of
us who have grown up in an epoch in which there is a virtually
superstitious respect for the sciences, as the purveyors of
trustworthy knowledge. No doubt Heidegger used the expression, 'Science does not think', partly with a view to the shock
effect of such words. He explains more fully what he has in mind
when he says that no matter where and however deeply science
investigates beings, it will never find Being.[4] For Heidegger, that
which is worthy to be called 'thinking' must have a relation to
Being. The sciences, as he believes, are concerned only with
beings, and dismiss 'Being' as nothing at all, or a mere philosophical fiction. Scientific thinking is classed by Heidegger as 'calculative' thinking, the kind of thinking that can be done by
computers.

Of course, one may say that he is grossly unfair to the scientist.
No doubt there is much 'calculative' thinking in the sciences, but
there are also the creative, imaginative moments of discovery,
events of unconcealedness, to use Heideggerian language. These
are surely major achievements of thought.

Likewise Heidegger excludes the theologian from the ranks of
the thinkers. For the true thinker, everything is – and remains –
problematical. But, in Heidegger's view, the theologian believes
that he has attained to secure knowledge through revelation. As I
have already indicated,[5] Heidegger has a curiously restricted
understanding of theology. In denying that the theologian is also
a thinker, he is contradicting his own pronouncement that 'there
is a *thinking* and questioning elaboration of the world of
Christian experience, that is, of faith,' that this enterprise is
theology, and that it has a 'true greatness'.

But we need not engage in arguments over the relative merits of
philosophy, science and theology. Let us rather go on and see
what more Heidegger has to tell us about the nature of thinking.
The first lecture course which Heidegger gave on being restored

to his teaching position at Freiburg after the period of suspension on account of his political activities was on this very subject of thinking. The material of this lecture course is difficult to understand, and even the title which Heidegger gave to it is open to various interpretations. In German, the title is, *Was heisst Denken?*. The English translation is known as *What Is Called Thinking?*[6]. Heidegger himself suggests four different ways of understanding this title. (1) ' "What is called thinking?" says in the first place, "What is it we call thought and thinking, what do these words signify? What is it to which we give the name thinking?" ' (2) ' "What is called thinking?" says also, in the second place, "How does the traditional doctrine conceive and define what we have named thinking? Why does the traditional doctrine of thinking bear the curious title logic?" ' (3) ' "What is called thinking?" says further, in the third place, "What are the prerequisites we need so that we may be able to think with essential rightness?" ' (4) ' "What is called thinking?" says in the fourth place, "What is it that calls us, as it were, commands us to think? What is it that calls us into thinking?" '[7] (It should be explained that the fourth way of formulating the question arises from an ambiguity in the German verb *heissen*. It can mean 'to bear a name', 'to be called', and that is the signification understood in the first three formulations. But it can also signify 'to command'. *Was heisst Denken* can mean 'What commands thinking', 'What calls forth thinking?' or 'What evokes thinking?' The fourth meaning is for Heidegger the important one.)

Heidegger had begun his course of lectures by saying: 'We come to know what it means to think when we ourselves try to think. If the attempt is to be successful, we must be ready to learn thinking. As soon as we allow ourselves to become involved in such learning, we have admitted that we are not yet capable of thinking.'[8] Thinking is certainly a possibility for the human being, this being has even been defined as the 'rational animal,' the finite being having the capability of thinking. Yet we are still not thinking!

Who are included in the 'we' who are not yet thinking? Is it contemporary society in general that constitutes the 'we'? Perhaps it is, for this is the age of science and technology, and we have already heard Heidegger's charge that science does not think. He believes that scientific thinking is calculative thinking, and we have also heard that for him the true thinking has a meditative character. As we shall see, it is more likely to be found among poets than among scientists, in Heidegger's view. But meditative thinking is responsive thinking. It is thinking that is called forth by that which is 'thought-provoking' (or thought-evoking). So we already begin to see why Heidegger regards as most important the fourth way of interpreting the question '*Was heisst Denken?*' – 'What calls forth thinking?' rather than 'What is called thinking?'. But perhaps the 'we' in 'we are not yet thinking' has a more restricted sense. It may refer to Heidegger himself and to those who are listening to his lecture or even to the philosophical community. Around this time, Heidegger was coming to believe that the great philosophical enterprise of Europe was coming to an end. In an essay with the somewhat apocalyptic title, 'The End of Philosophy and the Task of Thinking'[9], he confesses that ever since 1930 he had been seeking to rethink the problematic of *Being and Time* in a more adequate way. In following the development of his thought, we have already seen how his reorientation involved a more direct encounter with Being rather than an indirect approach to the question of Being through a preliminary study of the human being. This has led him into a new way of thinking, a thinking which is no longer the phenomenological investigation that he considered appropriate in *Being and Time*, but a meditative type of thought which is responsive to the thought-evoking influence of Being. Of course, this new way is also in some respects a repossessing of the origins of western thought, the insight of early thinkers, such as Parmenides, whose saying about thinking and being[10] has obviously had a great influence on Heidegger. To come back for a moment to the title of the essay, 'The End of Philosophy and the Task of Thinking', this title is not simply apocalyptic, for the final words about the task of thinking suggest that there is something that thinking can do even if traditional philosophy runs into the sand. This would be a new beginning, comparable, one may suppose, to the new beginning which may be possible through art when the current obsession with technology has run its course. Heidegger himself seems to suggest the parallel. He remarks that the carpenter responds to wood, in some such way as the thinker responds to that which evokes thought; but where in modern industry, he asks, is there anything comparable to the carpenter and his wood?[11]

The transition from the phenomenology of the existential analytic to the meditative thinking on Being is the core of that turn (*Kehre*) which students of Heidegger have noted. It is also, presumably, the reason for his beginning to speak of himself as a thinker, rather than a philosopher. But thinking and Being are so closely related in *Dasein* that if we begin with the one we are led to the other. Yet it would seem too that there is no direct way over from one to the other. 'Every philosophical – that is, thoughtful – doctrine of man's essential nature is *in itself alone* a doctrine of the Being of beings. Every doctrine of Being is *in itself alone* a doctrine of man's essential nature. But neither doctrine can be obtained by merely turning the other one around. No way of thought, not even the way of metaphysical thought, begins with man's essential nature and goes on from there to Being, nor in reverse from Being and then back to man. Rather, every way of thinking takes its way already within the total relation of Being and man's nature.'[12]

In the further elucidation of what it means to think, Heidegger relies to a large extent on linguistic considerations. When we come to his teaching on language, we shall examine his methods more closely and attempt an evaluation. Meanwhile, we shall attend to what he has to say about thinking and his answers to the four formulations of the question, 'What is called thinking?'.

One has first to listen to the language, to attend to the actual words. A whole family of German words come to mind: *denken* ('think'), *Gedanke* ('thought'), *Gedächtnis* ('memory'). With the exception of 'memory', which we have borrowed from Latin, the English words in this family are obviously cognate with the German ones and presumably have a similar semantic history. Closely connected with these words are the German *danken* and its English equivalent 'thank'; to thank someone is to have that person in one's memory and to think gratefully of him. Heidegger asks: 'Is thinking a giving of thanks? What do thanks mean here?

or do thanks consist in thinking? What does thinking mean here?'
The memory is not just a container for thoughts, and thoughts are
not just ideas and opinions. The relation to thanking shows us an
original sense of thinking, which Heidegger explicitly compares
with Pascal's famous teaching that the heart has its reasons,
something that Pascal tried to retrieve in the face of mathematical
thinking, which was coming into the ascendant.

In this part of his discussion, Heidegger resorts to a religious or
quasi-religious type of language. 'In giving thanks, the heart gives
thought to what it has and what it is. The heart, thus giving
thought and thus being memory, gives itself in thought to that to
which it is held. It thinks of itself as beholden, not in the sense of
mere submission, but beholden because its devotion is held in
listening. Original thanking is the thanks owed for being.'[13]

These remarks on thinking, memory and thanking, help to
explain Heidegger's answer to the question, 'What is called
thinking?' in the first and fourth of the four ways in which that
question may be understood.

A true thinking is more than an intellectual operation, it is a
disposition infused with thankfulness. This disposition is addressed to that which is above all thought-worthy and thought-
evoking. To quote: 'How can we give thanks for this gift, the gift
of being able to think what is most thought-evoking, more
fittingly than by giving thought to the most thought-evoking?'
Thinking therefore is for Heidegger close to worship, and the
expression, the 'piety of thinking' is not misplaced when applied
to him.[14]

Now the second way of understanding the question, 'What is
called thinking?' asked about its meaning in the tradition of
Western thought. This tradition, especially in modern times,
seems very different from what Heidegger has been talking about.
Pascal, it seems, lost his battle to maintain the reasons of the heart
as against the omnicompetent rationalism of the Renaissance and
the Enlightenment. For the mainstream of philosophical thinking
(the one which Heidegger thinks is drying up) took its clue about
the essential nature of thinking not from the German words
denken/danken but from the Greek Logos, and it made 'logic' the
yardstick for thinking. This is a different and independent

tradition, and it is obviously the one that has been essential for the rise of Western science and technology. It obviously has its own right, and no one can reject it, not even the sceptic or the deconstructionist who, in abolishing truth and logic, thereby abolishes also his or her own claim to be heard as a serious disputant. How this other tradition of thinking can be reconciled with the one advocated by Heidegger, or if it can be so reconciled, is a question that remains unanswered. Perhaps that is why Heidegger warned us that we have not yet attained to thinking, that is to say, thinking in its fullness, thinking as a part of our human experience in time, not as what Bradley once called a 'ballet of bloodless categories'.

We have then Heidegger's answers to the first, second and fourth senses of the question, 'What is called thinking?'. He does not appear to give any clear answer to the third form of the question, which asked about the prerequisites for correct thinking. Perhaps that is a question that could only be answered after we had learned how to reconcile the two understandings of thinking set out in the answers to the first and second formulations.

Before we can leave the topic of thinking, there is one other writing to which we must pay attention. This is the short book published in 1959 with the German title *Gelassenheit*. The book takes up again the theme of thinking, and this is reflected in the title of the English translation, *Discourse on Thinking*.[15]

The word *Gelassenheit* is difficult to translate into English, and whatever translation one uses, it will be unsatisfactory in one way or another. In the published English translation, *Gelassenheit* is rendered by 'releasement', though this is not a recognized English word and will not be found even in good dictionaries. 'Collectedness', 'calmness', 'serenity' are other possible equivalents, though they miss the sense of separation or even abandonment. Another possibility is 'detachment', something like the *Abgeschiedenheit* of Meister Eckhart, and *Gelassenheit* does have mystical associations. In the following brief discussion of this text, I shall not feel bound exclusively to any one translation of the term *Gelassenheit*.

Once more we are told that in the contemporary world there is a flight from thinking. This is true in spite of all the research that goes on. For (so Heidegger believes) this research takes the form of calculative thinking. He claims: 'Calculative thinking races from one prospect to the next. Calculative thinking never stops, never collects itself. Calculative thinking is not meditative thinking, not thinking which contemplates the meaning which reigns in everything that is.'[16] If we are to attain to that collectedness or peace of mind denoted by the term *Gelassenheit*, we must cultivate this other thinking, meditative thinking.

So far the message is much the same as we have heard in *What Is Called Thinking*. But what seems to be new in the text now being considered is the special stress laid on the idea that thinking is not primarily a human activity but an activity induced in man or even infused into man by a reality beyond the human – what in the earlier treatise on thinking was called the 'Thought-provoking' or the 'Thought-evoking'. In *Discourse on Thinking*, we seem to reach the furthest remove from that bold Promethean moment in *Being and Time* when *Dasein* expresses joy in the freedom of facing death without illusions.[17] Now we are told that joy or peace of mind is not something willed by *Dasein* through resoluteness but a gift that is offered. Let me quote two or three sentences from the conversation of a scholar, a teacher and a scientist which forms part of the text of *Discourse on Thinking*:

> Scholar: So far as we can wean ourselves from willing, we contribute to the awakening of releasement.
> Teacher: Say rather, to keeping awake for releasement.
> Scholar: Why not, to the awakening?
> Teacher: Because on our own we do not awaken releasement in ourselves.
> Scientist: Thus releasement is effected from somewhere else?
> Teacher: Not effected, but let in.

Are we then simply dependent on something beyond ourselves, so that we can only wait and hope for releasement to be let in? This, it is said, would be a poor consolation. Presumably, we can prepare ourselves and open ourselves. The problem raised here is rather like the theological one of divine grace. Does the human being surrender his or her own will completely, which would seem to imply becoming less than human, a mere puppet? Or must there be some responsive acceptance or appropriation on the human side, some element of 'synergism', to use the theological term? Something like this seems to be hinted when it is said that the attainment of releasement is neither active nor passive, but somehow beyond that distinction.[18]

But the apparently anthropocentric emphasis of *Being and Time* is now explicitly abandoned, though Heidegger here, as in some other places, gives the impression that he is reinterpreting the earlier passage rather than moving on to a quite new and different view of the matter. What he actually says is: 'One needs to understand "resolve" as it is understood in *Being and Time*: as the opening of *Dasein particularly* undertaken by him *for* openness.'[19]

We move on from thinking to language, and this can be treated more briefly since some of the questions replicate those already met in the discussion of thinking. Although Heidegger seems to believe that some thinking is possible without being expressed in language, most of our thinking does require language, and the two are intimately connected.

Already in *Being and Time* Heidegger was showing his interest in language, or, to speak more accurately, in discourse (*Rede*). Discourse is placed alongside understanding and disposition as one of the major *existentialia* or basic characteristics of *Dasein*.[20] As time went on, Heidegger attached more and more importance to language. Of course, already in *Being and Time*, apart from his explicit remarks on discourse and its inauthentic manifestation as 'idle talk', Heidegger in his philosophical method was implicitly making use of ideas about language and the importance of words for philosophical understanding. We shall come back to this shortly.

In its general direction, Heidegger's teaching about language follows a path roughly parallel to what he says about thinking, that is to say, the focus moves from the human activity to a source beyond man in Being or whatever other expression may be used for the comprehensive reality within which humanity has its place. Already in his *Introduction to Metaphysics*, Heidegger sees language as not a human instrument or a human invention, but as a pervading presence of Being in the finite human being. In discussing a chorus from Sophocles,[21] he writes: 'How far man is from being at home in his own essence is revealed by his opinion of himself as he who invented and could have invented language and understanding, building and poetry. How could man ever have invented the power which pervades him, which alone enables him to *be* a man?' In language and thinking Heidegger sees the mysterious connection between *Dasein* and Being – a connection which, he believes, was first seen among Western thinkers by Parmenides, whose saying about being and thinking he never tires of repeating.[22]

The dependence of human speech on the gift of Being is repeated in the *Letter on Humanism*. 'Before he speaks, man must first let himself be addressed (or claimed) again by Being, with the risk that when so addressed, he will seldom have much to say. Only thus will the preciousness of its essence be once more bestowed upon the word, and upon man a home for dwelling in the truth of Being.'[23] It is in this writing too that we first find language itself described as the 'house of Being', an expression which will occupy us later.

Heidegger's fullest treatment of language is the book *Unterwegs zur Sprache* or, in the English translation, *On the Way to Language*. The German edition appeared in 1959, and consists of six essays, written between 1950 and 1958. In this book, language, like thinking, is seen as making an essential connection between *Dasein* and Being. 'The capacity for speech', we are told, 'is not just one power of the human being alongside others; it is what distinguishes the human being as human.'[24] Already in *Being and Time*, the point had been made that the philosophical definition of man as *zoon logon echon* should be translated not as the 'rational animal' but more fully as 'that living thing whose being is essentially determined by the potentiality for discourse'.[25] So speech is made the essential mark of the human being. At the same time, language is given an essential place in the structure of Being as such. 'The being of everything that is dwells in the word. Hence the validity of the statement, "Language is the house of Being".'[26] Does this mean that Being itself comes to speech in human language?

Obviously there is much in Heidegger that hinges on this deep connection that language is alleged to provide between *Dasein* and Being. Does language provide, as it were, an ancient memory of *Dasein*'s origin from and kinship with Being? (Here we may think of what he has said about thinking, memory and gratitude.) Or does an understanding of Being already lie hidden in the depths of language? (Here we may recall that at the beginning of *Being and Time*, Heidegger suggests that we could not raise the question of Being unless we already had some understanding of the meaning of Being, however vague it might be.)[27]

If there is any possibility of answering these questions affirmatively, then there would seem to be some justification for Heidegger's frequent appeals to language and the supposed original meanings of words and their etymological connections, in the working out of his philosophy. Language would indeed be the 'house of Being', a kind of treasure house in which are hidden all the riches of God. And it would justify the claim that there is a thinking which listens and is open for a word of God.

But these are highly controversial matters, and it must be confessed that some of Heidegger's etymologies are speculative, and that he is by no means consistent in his appeals. For instance, if we take the important Greek word Logos, literally 'word' or 'discourse', he tells us in *Being and Time* that *logos* means the same as *deloun*, 'to make manifest', and he uses this identification to elucidate the meaning of phenomeno*logy*.[28] In *Introduction to Metaphysics*, he takes a different line. The word *logos* and the related verb *legein*, 'to speak', did not, he claims, originally refer to speech. Their original meaning was that of gathering or collecting, as we see also in the cognate German verb *lesen*, 'to gather' and also 'to read'. A gatherer of wood in the Black Forest is a *Holzleser*.[29] If we move on to *What Is Called Thinking* we find a third explanation of *logos* and *legein*. Now Heidegger tells us that these words are cognate with the German verb *legen*, 'to lay' or 'to let lie'. He translates a saying of Parmenides, '*chre to legein . . .*' as 'Useful is the letting-lie-before-us . . .'[30] I do not say that Heidegger could not if required produce evidence in favour of all three ways of interpreting *logos*, but it is hard not to be sceptical or even to suspect that his translations are to some extent made to conform to his own philosophical position.

Further doubts arise when one considers linguistic points which he makes concerning the centrality of the problem of Being. It is true that 'we' can utter scarcely a couple of sentences without using some part of the verb 'to be', and this would seem to imply that we have some understanding of what it means 'to be', though we might find it difficult to say exactly what it is. But we have to ask, 'Who are "we" who claim this understanding?'. The answer is that we are speakers of Indo-European languages. When he writes a chapter on 'The Grammar and Etymology of the Word "Being"' in his *Introduction to Metaphysics*, the discussion covers only German and Greek. Admittedly, he does suggest that German and Greek are the only possible languages for any worthwhile philosophy. Still, not everyone would agree. And what about Semitic languages, or even an Indo-European language like Russian, where the word 'is' is rarely if ever used? Perhaps 'being' is implied or thought in everything we say, as St Thomas suggested.[31] But to show this would require more than linguistic evidence.

Incidentally, Heidegger's attempts to derive philosophical points from etymological or other linguistic considerations may be compared to the fascination of some Anglo-Saxon philosophers with 'ordinary language'. However differently Heidegger and these English-speaking philosophers apply the principle, they seem to be agreed that there are hidden stores of wisdom in the way we talk. Yet on both sides there is agreement that language is very fallible and may conceal more than it reveals.

The text of *Unterwegs zur Sprache* contains a number of autobiographical allusions, some of which are relevant to our own special interest in Heidegger's relation to Christianity and theology. One of the pieces records a conversation between Heidegger and a Japanese scholar. In the course of it, Heidegger, recalling his early linguistic and hermeneutical studies in the seminary, frankly admits: 'Without my theological origins, I would never have attained to the path of thinking.'[32] Later in the same conversation, the Japanese visitor tells him, 'For us, the void (*das Leere*) is the highest name for what you call Being.'[33] This remark raises the question of Heidegger's relation to mysticism, and also helps to explain why, in Japan, he has never been suspected of nihilism.

It will be remembered that when we considered Heidegger's view of the fine arts and the part which they might play in renewing *Dasein* when threatened by the constrictions of his own technology, we learned that he believed poetry to have first place among the arts.[34] Now that we have attended to what he says about language, we are in a position to turn to poetry as that particular form of language which in a signal way lights up Being.

Some preliminary remarks need to be made. Back in the eighteenth century, the eccentric German man of letters, Johann Georg Hamann (1730–88) put forward the theory (not widely held nowadays) that the most primitive human language was poetry. 'Poetry is the mother-tongue of the human race, as the garden is older than the field, painting than writing, song than declamation, parables than inferences, barter than commerce.'[35] Heidegger seems to have accepted this theory, at least during one period of his life. Obviously it fitted well with his own belief that the beginning of something like language has a greatness which soon gets lost and which we must try to recapture in a repetition or retrieving of the creative moment.[36] Some such ideas lie behind his claim that 'primitive language is poetry, in which being is established'.[37] The emergence of *Dasein* as a temporal and historical being depends on language, especially poetic language.

However, although Heidegger sometimes speaks as if he was referring to poetry in general, he was in fact mainly taken up with the poetry of one man – Friedrich Hölderlin (1770–1843). This German poet, a contemporary of Hegel, had been stricken in his thirties by schizophrenia, and he was virtually ignored during his lifetime and for the rest of the nineteenth century. But, like Kierkegaard, he was discovered in the twentieth century, especially after the publication of his collected poems in 1913.[38] Heidegger was among those attracted, even fascinated, by Hölderlin. Why was this so? Perhaps the first reason was that Hölderlin had explicitly testified to the same understanding of the poet's role as Heidegger was reaching toward in his studies of thought and language. Heidegger declares that Hölderlin was, 'in a pre-eminent sense, the poet of the poet', that is to say, the poet who reflected upon and expounded how he understood his own activity as a poet. He saw secondly the poet as a kind of intermediary between the gods and men. We shall consider shortly what this implies. A third reason was that Hölderlin in his poetry was reading the present phase of history in the West in a way close to Heidegger's own way. Both men were unwilling to go along with Nietzsche's assertion that 'God is dead', but were aware of the absence of God in the modern age, attributing this, however, to his withdrawal, rather than to his demise. A fourth point is that both Hölderlin and Heidegger had a virtually unlimited admiration for the Greeks, and for the rise among them of the original impulses of Western culture and civilization. It may be significant too that both men were at one time theological students. Towards the end of his life, Hölderlin's poems were moving away from Hellenic toward Christian values. Whether something similar would be true of Heidegger is a point that we have yet to consider. But now let me try to spell out these points more fully by illustrating them from some passages in Hölderlin's poetry, and, where appropriate, from Heidegger's comments on that poetry.

On the first point, let me quote two lines from a very late writing of Hölderlin, which had to be edited by an intimate companion when the poet's mind was confused:

Voll Verdienst, doch dichterisch wohnet
  Der Mensch auf dieser Erde.

It is not easy to render this into English. Obviously, a contrast is intended between the first two words and the rest of the sentence. I think it would be true to Hölderlin's intentions to translate as follows:

Though he has to earn a living,
  Man dwells poetically on this earth.

What does this mean? It means that for most of his or her time, a human being will be engaged in what Heidegger would call 'everyday' existence, that is to say, the routine affairs of work and business. But for a truly human life, something more is needed, what is here called the 'poetic' dimension in which things are seen in the light of Being, in their intrinsic truth and beauty. The difference between the two experiences can be expressed as a difference in the experience of temporality and time. When poetry (or a language approaching to poetry) comes into play, time ceases to be a series of unrelated or only externally related 'nows' – the past is preserved and through its return in meditation or memory (*Andenken*) swings over our present and comes to us as future.[39] So we become temporal beings, living in the three 'ecstases' of past, present and future. This, we are told, is what makes history possible (as the repetition of authentic possibility) and this argument does not seem to depend on Hamann's theory of language.

On the second point, Hölderlin's poem 'Homecoming' is particularly enlightening. The poet has been abroad and now comes home. We see him crossing over Lake Constance from Switzerland to his native Germany. This is the pattern of the poet's existence – he must leave his native place, sojourn abroad, and then return to share what he has learned. Hölderlin literally made that kind of journey, but the pattern can be understood allegorically. For both Hölderlin and Heidegger, the poet is a go-between – he converses with the gods and then comes back with his message to the people. This is the same pattern that we see in prophets and founders of religions – a revelation, perhaps in itself ineffable, which the bearers break down into language. In Heidegger and Hölderlin, the function is transferred to poets. They operate in the region *between* gods and men. It is a hard existence, to be exposed to the heavenly fire, and then to bring it to one's fellows:

> Yet it behoves us, under the storms of God,
> Ye poets! with uncovered head to stand,
> With our own hand to grasp the Father's lightning-flash

And to pass on, wrapped in song,
The divine gift to the people.

But what seems to be missing in this poetic account of revelation
is any ethical content. The poets names the holy, opens up truth
and beauty, but where is the call to righteousness and love that we
find in Jesus or Moses or Mohammed or the Buddha?

On the third point, the signs of the times, especially the absence
of God, we go to Hölderlin's poem 'Bread and Wine' for a
striking statement:

But, friends, we have come too late! The gods are, indeed, alive,
But above our heads, up there in another world.
There they are endlessly active, and seem to heed little
Whether we are alive: that's how much the heavenly ones care.

We recognize here something close to Heidegger's own teaching.
God is not dead, but he has withdrawn himself. We shall come
back to this point in the next chapter.

The fourth and last point concerned the strongly Hellenic
colouring of thought in both Hölderlin and Heidegger. Who are
the 'gods' who have departed, and who are the coming 'gods'?
Presumably not literally Zeus, Apollo, Poseidon and the rest. Of
course, beyond the Greek gods was *moira*, and perhaps beyond
what Heidegger calls God or the gods is Being, as a kind of
destining. He can also say that the Holy is older than the gods.
'The holy is not holy because it is divine, but the divine is divine
because it is "holy" in a way proper to itself.' This may remind us
of the enigmatic question about the meaning of 'God' in the
Letter on Humanism.[40] But does not this strong Hellenism, and
the idea of some ultimate beyond God make Heidegger finally
incompatible with Christian thought? In reply, I would say that
we cannot jump to conclusions too quickly. There have been
Christian thinkers, not all of them mystics, who have thought
that behind what we call by the much abused name of 'God'
there is a Godhead beyond our conceptuality. Dionysius the
Areopagite talked of a 'God beyond God', and so more recently

did Paul Tillich. Even the great catholic theologian, Karl Rahner, sometimes refers to God as the Nameless or Ineffable. We can pursue the question only when we have thought about the phrase Heidegger used frequently toward the end of his life: 'Only a God can save us!'

7

'Only a God Can Save Us'

In the earlier chapters of this book, we have followed the train of Heidegger's thought from its beginnings in the days when he was a student at Freiburg, then during the period of his own teaching in Marburg and Freiburg. There was an interruption of five years after World War II when he was suspended from teaching because of his involvements with National Socialism in the 1930s. But this involvement was not judged to be of the serious 'active' kind, and in 1950 he returned to his professorial duties and during the next decade was very productive. He reached retiring age in 1959, but even after that he continued to write and lecture. It is this final phase of his work that we shall consider in the present chapter.

The words which stand as the title of this chapter, 'Only a God Can Save Us', (*Noch nur ein Gott kann uns retten*) are said to have been uttered quite frequently by Heidegger during this time, and they eventually formed the title for an article in the respected German news magazine, *Der Spiegel*, an article which was taken to be Heidegger's final communication. It will demand a close examination later. Meanwhile, it is enough to say that the title of this article does not tell us very much in itself. The urgency of the words is understandable, for the world was still immersed in the 'Cold War' and in late 1962 the Cuban missile crisis brought us to the very edge of a nuclear conflict between the United States and the Soviet Union. Probably many other people besides Heidegger were thinking that only a God could save the human race from self-destruction. But how many of these people would understand the words in the same sense as Heidegger? We have indeed seen that from his early Catholicism he moved through something close to a nihilistic atheism to a philosophical stance which, to judge from the vocabulary he used, seemed to be in process of becoming more religious. But at this point we cannot say more than 'seemed'.

What, for instance, does Heidegger mean by 'God' when he says, 'Only a God can save us'? It would be naive to assume that by the word 'God' he understands what most Christian theologians would understand by 'God'. We remember that while he criticized Sartre for hastily embracing atheism, he said of himself that he was neither an atheist nor a theist.[1] When Heidegger does use the word 'God,' he often does so in a hypothetical manner, so that, for instance, when he speaks of God as temporal, the sentence should be interpreted, 'If there is a God, then he is temporal', or perhaps, 'The idea of God in Christian or Jewish faith is that of a God who is temporal.'

Many writers, especially theologians who have been attracted by Heidegger's thinking, have searched through his works for a conception of God. A good example of this is the substantial volume *Heidegger et la Question de Dieu*.[2] The authors of this volume, who are mainly Catholic in outlook, do not reach any agreed conclusions, and indeed it was not to be expected that they would. I have myself searched for a concept of God in Heidegger, but could reach only tentative conclusions,[3] but I shall repeat these in the present volume, adducing additional reasons for thinking that they may at least point in the right direction.

It must be stressed, however, that there is no possibility of a neat summing up of some so-called Heideggerian philosophy at the end of a study of his work. That would be quite contrary to his own intentions as a thinker. He aimed not at a rounded philosophy but at following a path of thinking, and that path sometimes turned out to be different from what he had expected. In some ways, like the country path close to Messkirch,[4] the path led back to the starting-point. We remember that Heidegger set out on the path of thinking inspired by Brentano's book *On the Several Senses of Being in Aristotle*.[5] Shortly before his death in 1976, writing a preface which he never finished to the planned complete edition of his works, Heidegger referred to those works as a stage in 'the changing questioning in the manifold question of Being'.[6] So it does seem here that the end is the beginning, or perhaps a new beginning, for Heidegger believed that the traditional philosophy, built around the concept of substance, had come to an end, but this is also the possibility of a new beginning, perhaps even the same beginning for which the presocratic thinkers were looking, before their work was set aside and the question of Being gave way to an exclusive interest in the beings.

In this chapter, our reflections will be concentrated on three works from the closing years of Heidegger's activity. 'Time and Being' is a fairly short piece, but it is of special interest because it obviously reverses the title of *Being and Time*, and though it does not fill the gap left by Heidegger's failure to complete that early book, it does make important contributions to two of the major questions that have been in our minds all through the course of this book – the question of time and temporality, and the question of God. This piece dates from 1962. The second piece is also short, but it has a very long title: 'The Theological Discussion of "The Problem of a Non-objectifying Thinking and Speaking in Today's Theology" – Some Pointers to its Major Aspects'. This piece was specially written by Heidegger for a conference of theologians held at Drew University, New Jersey. I had the privilege of being present myself on that occasion, but once again, as you will see when I report on it below, the end seems to have brought us once again to the beginning – or maybe a new beginning. This piece belongs to the year 1964. Finally, there is the article from *Der Spiegel*, which I have already briefly mentioned. This article reports an interview with two journalists, given by Heidegger in 1966, on condition that it would not be published until after his death. Publication therefore duly took place in 1976, and this article may be fairly regarded as Heidegger's last public word.

Let us first look then at Heidegger's lecture, 'Time and Being'.[7] He begins by warning us of the difficulty of the task. If we look at a painting by Paul Klee, we are not likely to understand it immediately. We need time to look at it, study it and think about it. Similarly, if someone reads us a poem by Georg Trakl, it will not immediately yield its meaning and we may have to spend quite a long time pondering it. In quite a different field, a discovery by Werner Heisenberg in theoretical physics would probably be unintelligible to the vast majority of people, and only a hard and sustained effort of thought will enable us to understand it. Should we expect matters to be any different in philosophy? Being and time, time and being—these are extremely elusive, and so is the relation between them. As we have heard from Heidegger during the whole time of his philosophizing, Being is not a thing, not itself a being, so that in strict grammar one cannot even say, 'Being is . . .' And what about time? Time is not a thing either. We say, everything has its time, but this is not some other thing that it has. Time and Being seem like insubstantial ghosts, non-beings. Perhaps we have to go back to Heidegger's 1929 lecture on 'nothing' before we try to understand what could be the relation between time and Being. Let us at least remind ourselves of some sentences from the postscript to that lecture: 'No matter where and however deeply science investigates beings, it will never find Being. All its encounters at any time are beings, because its explanatory purpose has been directed from the outset to beings. But Being is not an existing quality of beings, nor, unlike beings, can Being be conceived and established objectively.'[8] Yet it is this non-entity that 'gives every entity the warrant (*Gewahr*) to be'.

Time seems even less substantial and harder to grasp than Being. Time is not a thing, but the medium, as we might say, in which things arise and pass away. In a sense, time itself passes away, but in another sense only the things in time pass away, while time remains as time.

As to the relation between time and Being, Heidegger fixes on the notion of presence. He claims that 'from the dawn of western or European thinking until today, Being means the same as presencing'.[9] Presence speaks of the present, so that Being is determined by time and time by Being. 'Being and time', says Heidegger, 'determine each other reciprocally, but in such a manner that neither can the former, Being, be addressed as something temporal, nor can the latter, time, be addressed as a being.'[10]

So Heidegger seems to be succeeding in slowing down our thinking, just as much as if we were trying to make sense of an abstract painting by Klee or puzzling over an obscure poem of

Trakl or trying to understand a formula of Heisenberg. His move out of the impasse is accomplished, or at least, attempted, by again recalling a point in his earlier thinking. We cannot say, 'Being is', or 'Time is', but we do say, 'There is Being' or 'There is time'. The expression, 'There is Being' takes us all the way back to *Being and Time*, and it was later elucidated in the *Letter on Humanism*.[11] In German, the words are *Es gibt*, 'It gives', and in capitalizing the *Es* and the 'It', I am following Heidegger's own example at this point. He remarks: 'We try to bring the It and its giving into view, and capitalize the "It".'[12] We are then to fix our attention on the 'It gives', which seems to be the source of both Being and time. 'It gives Being' means that there is presence, that there is unconcealment, that *Dasein* is brought into the clearing. Here Heidegger has to strain language to the uttermost, and one is left wondering whether something very important has been said or whether we are simply adrift. 'To think Being explicitly,' he claims, 'requires us to relinquish Being as the ground of beings in favour of the giving . . . that is, in favour of the "It gives".' I shall not go on quoting Heidegger's somewhat tortuous language, but suggest an analogy that may help to make his point clearer. To those who find the language of theology more familiar, it is as if some one were to say, 'To think explicitly of God, you must think of him in abstraction from all created things,' or, to put it in another way, try to think of an act of pure creating, apart from any creature that is created. This would be to think the ontological difference between Being and beings, or, theologically expressed, the difference between God and the *ens creatum*. Can the human being attain such a level of thought? Perhaps the mystic can in some ecstatic flight. Perhaps Plotinus did, perhaps Eckhart did, perhaps even Heidegger did. I do not have to decide about these questions, I am simply reporting what I believe Heidegger was teaching. He says clearly that Being is a gift of the 'It gives' and that Being belongs to giving. The 'It gives' is the ultimate in Heidegger's philosophy. Perhaps we can say some things about it, but we seem to have come to the source and exactly what this 'It' is, we cannot say — we cannot even say that it 'is'.

To find a parallel to the kind of language used by Heidegger concerning Being, we have to go back to the neo-Platonists, and I have argued elsewhere[13] that broadly speaking, Heidegger stands in the neo-Platonist tradition. What Heidegger says about the status of Being is remarkably similar to what Eruigena says about God. Eruigena used of God the adjective 'superessential'. 'It says that it is not essence but more than essence, but what that is which is more than essence, it does not reveal. For it says that God is not one of the things that are, but that he is more than the things that are; but what that "is" is, it in no way defines.'[14] Perhaps the link between Heidegger and neo-Platonism is to be found in Meister Eckhart, or perhaps it was established earlier when Heidegger was immersed in mediaeval thought. When we were considering the *Letter on Humanism*, it seemed to me that at the time it was written, Being was, for Heidegger, if not God, then a surrogate for God, for the language used in respect of Being was very much like the language of religion. Thus, although Heidegger explicitly says in the *Letter* that Being is not God, one might argue that Being has taken the place of God. Since Heidegger himself claims that violence is permissible in hermeneutics, he could hardly object if some of his readers claimed to find in his writings meanings which he did not wish them to find. But it is the 'It gives' that is more ultimate even than Being and seems to come close to what has ordinarily been understood as God. In Christian theology, God is love. In Heidegger, 'It gives' is an act of giving or donation, and since he has told us that the 'It' which gives Being is Being itself, then the act of giving is also an act of self-giving, and so not different in any major respect from love.

Whether the 'It gives' is different from Being is debatable. 'It gives' is an act and has primarily a verbal sense, whereas Being is a noun, though a verbal noun. The verbal sense is important and is in agreement with Heidegger's desire to get away from the notion of substance as the supreme category. It also agrees with the idea that even the ultimate reality may be in some sense temporal.

These remarks may shed some light on Heidegger's declaration that he is neither a theist nor an atheist.[15] He is not a theist if we limit that description to a God who is personal, substantial, and above or beyond time. But if we are willing to say that God is suprapersonal, that he is an event rather than a substance, and that in some respects at least he is temporal, then one might claim that in this broad sense, Heidegger's philosophy is theistic. I am inclined to agree with John R. Williams that '"panentheism" accords well with the elements in Heidegger's thought that are relevant to religion'.[16] But to some extent this is a question of names and labels, and we have seen that Heidegger cared little about labels when he addressed those who were concerned about the future of 'humanism'.

Even the name of God or the designation as 'theist' of a believer in God is not perhaps of the highest importance. 'God' is indeed the primary reality for Christianity, Judaism, Islam and various other religions. But then, there are also religions, especially in Asia, for which the word 'God' has not such a central place. These religions centre no less than the specifically theistic ones on what I call 'holy Being' and it is, I think, this recognition of a holy or sacred reality at the heart of all being that is essential to religion and makes the significant difference between religion and a true atheism. If anyone wishes to deny that Heidegger's thought has any room for God, that seems to me to be a question of terminology. What cannot be denied is that enshrined in that thought is a holy reality.

'In the beginning of western thinking, Being is thought, but not the "It gives" as such. The latter withdraws in favour of the gift which It gives.'[17] This explains 'the forgetting of Being' in Western thought, which, according to Heidegger, began at a very early stage. From then on, western *Dasein* has been immersed in the beings and its thinking dominated by ideas of substantiality and presence-at-hand. This was also the cause of the rise of metaphysics. *Dasein* has been in search of a ground, a firm thinglike reality under its feet. Heidegger and Kant were both suspicious of metaphysics, but both acknowledged that the human being is incurably metaphysical. But whereas Kant the rationalist attributed the metaphysical urge to intellectual curiosity, Heidegger saw its motivation in the historical insecurity of *Dasein*.

Some further remarks need to be made about the lecture 'Time and Being'. Can we learn any more about the mysterious 'It gives', from which, it would seem, come Being and all else? At least, we learn a name for it, though this in itself may not be much. 'What determines both time and Being in their own, that is, in their belonging together, we shall call *Ereignis*, the event of appropriation.'[18] So this ultimate source is not a substance but an event, as indeed is clear from the name we have already learned, 'It gives'. But it is an event of 'appropriation'. What does that mean? The German verb *ereignen* usually means simply 'to happen', while the noun *Ereignis* is simply 'event'. But in using such words, Heidegger is again exploiting their etymology and drawing attention to relationships usually left unobserved, yet which lie deep in language and presumably in thinking. *Ereignis* includes the root *eigen* corresponding to the English word 'own'. This word *eigen* is, of course, also met in the word *eigentlich*, which we have translated 'authentic', as when we speak of an 'authentic existence'. The *Ereignis* then is not just any event, but the event of appropriation, when something is made someone's own. This appropriation would seem to be the other side of the act of giving. So we read: 'The gift of presence is the property of appropriating'.[19] But almost immediately we are warned that sometimes instead of the granting of a presence there may be a withdrawal, and we shall see later what this means. But meantime we are concerned with presence and presencing rather than withdrawal. To what does Being present itself? Obviously, to *Dasein*, the being who is a clearing, the locus where the light gets through, the one who has access to unconcealedness, to being in the truth. The idea of an event of appropriation therefore gathers together many items in Heidegger's thinking. It is an illustration of Logos, which Heidegger understands as 'gathering'.

We now pass to the second of the three late writings of Heidegger which are to be discussed in this chapter. This was the piece which Heidegger wrote for a theological conference at Drew University, New Jersey, in early 1964, on the problem of a non-objectifying thinking and speaking in theology.[20] It had been hoped that Heidegger himself would attend the conference, but in fact he decided only to send the paper.

Presumably he was invited because there is something like a parallel between the God-language of the theologian and the Being-language of Heidegger. Many modern theologians, such as Tillich and Bultmann, insist that God is not an entity that we can objectify in our thought, and that we know God only in certain kinds of experience as demand (Bultmann), depth (Tillich), the holy (Otto). Heidegger, on his side, tells us that Being 'is' not a being and cannot be objectified, and is known through such experiences as *Angst* or anxiety. So perhaps the theologians were hoping that Heidegger could help them in their quest for an intelligible language about God.

On the whole, it must be said that the theologians were disappointed. In his remarks on theology in 1964, Heidegger did not appear to be saying anything very different from what he had said in that early lecture on theology in 1927 – namely, that theology and philosophy are quite different enterprises and that theologians must solve their own problems and will only cause trouble for themselves if they introduce ideas from philosophy.

Heidegger sees three questions that need to be considered:

1. What is theology itself to have as its subject-matter? He answers this question much as he had done forty years earlier. Theology is concerned with the exposition of Christian faith, and must find ways of speaking and thinking that correspond to the claims of faith and do not project alien ideas into it.[21] This is something for the theologians themselves to decide.

2. Before we begin to talk about *non*-objectifying thought or language, it is necessary to ask what is intended by the adjective 'objectifying' and then to ask whether all language and speaking are objectifying. If all language is objectifying, then the whole problem collapses.

3. In view of what has just been said, one must decide whether we have not got into a pseudo-problem which 'only circumvents the matter, diverts from the theme of theology and unnecessarily confounds it'.[22] This might indicate that the conference had entered a blind alley, but Heidegger believes one positive result might emerge – 'that theology [might] once and for all get clear about the requisite of its major task not to borrow the categories of its thinking and the form of its speech from philosophy or the sciences, but to think and speak out of faith for faith with fidelity to its subject-matter. If this faith by the power of its own conviction concerns man as man in his very nature, then genuine theological thinking and speaking have no need of a special resource (*Zurüstung*) to reach people and find a hearing among them.'[23]

Heidegger then tells us that he is going to give some 'pointers' toward answering the second of the three questions, but he wants to make it clear that his remarks are not 'dogmatic theses stated in terms of a Heideggerian philosophy, when there is no such thing'.

Objectifying thinking is something which we have already seen Heidegger criticizing in his earlier writings. In such thinking, things and even people are so many items set before us for observation or possibly for manipulation, present-at-hand or ready-to-hand in Heidegger's terminology. Heidegger points out that in modern philosophy there is a tension concerning this matter of thinking and speaking that in some ways is similar to the difficulties that the theologian may have with God-language. The tension in philosophy (Heidegger was writing in 1964) was between one extreme, represented by Rudolf Carnap, who held that all meaningful language is in principle reducible to the language of physics, and another extreme, represented by Heidegger himself, which allows a much wider range of meaningful language. Heidegger called these two extremes, the technical-scientist view of language, and the speculative-hermeneutical experience of language. Both positions hold that language is the realm within which all philosophical and other thinking takes place. 'It is up to theology to decide in what manner and to what extent it can and should enter into this debate'[24] – a debate which, it is said has to do not just with language but with the whole question of human existence.

This objectifying language, of which the extreme manifestations are physicalism and logical positivism, had been taking shape for a long time, though it had been challenged before Heidegger by such philosophers as Nietzsche and Bergson. Both of them had stressed the importance of 'becoming' which cannot be adequately expressed in a language which takes substance or thinghood as its governing category. Heidegger claims further that proof and demonstration, whether by verification or by some other means, though appropriate in some cases, is not so in others. 'To think critically means to distinguish constantly between that which requires proof for its justification and that which, to confirm its truth, demands simple catching sight of it and taking it in.'[25] This is, of course, his own doctrine of truth as unconcealment. Heidegger is in no way denying the procedures of the natural sciences, but he does claim that 'there is a thinking and saying that is in no manner objectified.' He immediately gives an example: 'The statue of Apollo at Olympia we can indeed regard as an object of natural-scientific representation; we can calculate the physical weight of the marble; we can investigate its chemical composition. But this objectifying thinking and speaking does not catch sight of the Apollo who shows forth his beauty and so appears as the visage of the god.'[26]

So Heidegger believes that 'the assertion that all thinking as thinking is objectifying is without foundation. It rests on a disregard of phenomena and betrays a lack of critique.'[27] But he sees a danger that in the present age of technology the objectifying mode of thinking and speaking will be extended to all areas of life, with bad consequences for both language and life.

Presumably his paper brought some comfort to the theologians and gave them some ideas for further discussion. But at the end of his paper, remarking that theology is certainly not a *natural* science, he wonders whether it is a science at all. Perhaps it is close to poetry, and perhaps his own philosophy is, in at least some of its aspects. For poetry, in Heidegger's view, is certainly not 'non-cognitive' but is, in his own words, 'an outstanding example of non-objective thinking'.

Finally we come to the article from *Der Spiegel*,[28] 'Only a God Can Save Us'. I have already explained the circumstances under which this was written, and suggested that it may be regarded as Heidegger's last word to his readers.

About half of the article is a kind of inquisition into Heidegger's relation to National Socialism, a subject which would obviously be of greater interest to most readers of the journal than difficult discussions of his philosophy. As already promised, these political questions will be discussed in the final chapter of this book. But later the conversation between Heidegger and the two journalists broadened out. Heidegger has expressed some of the misgivings he had about the technical age and complained that the human being is in process of being uprooted from the earth. (Let us remember that this conversation was taking place while the Cold War was still at its height.) One of the journalists puts to him the question whether philosophy can do anything to help. 'Can any individual influence the network of forces that are controlling us, or can philosophy influence it, or can both together have an influence, with the philosophy of an individual or a group of individuals leading us to definite action?' Heidegger replies: 'If I may make a short and general reply, but one that comes from long pondering, philosophy can effect no immediate change in the present state of the world. This holds not only for philosophy, but for all merely human intelligence and endeavour. Now only a God can save us. The only possibility remaining to us is that in thinking and in poetry there can be prepared a readiness for the appearing of the God, or for the absence of the God in a decline: that we decline in face of the absent God.'

> Journalist: 'Is there a connection between your thinking and the coming of this God? Is there, in your view, a causal connection? Do you mean that we can by thinking bring the God near?'
> Heidegger: 'We cannot bring him near by thinking, at best, we can awaken the readiness to expect him.'
> Journalist: 'But can we help?'
> Heidegger: 'Preparing the readiness might be the first step in helping. The world cannot be what and how it is through human beings, but neither can it without human beings. That depends, in my view, on whether something that I call by a traditional but ambiguous and worn out word, "Being", requires man for its revelation, preservation and articulation.'

Let us pause at this point to consider what Heidegger has been saying. Something like an eschatological note has come in – the readiness for the advent of a God. But this word 'God' is ambiguous in the present context. It seems hardly likely that Heidegger means the God of Christian faith, though this is not impossible. But I say 'hardly likely', because, as we have seen, Heidegger seemed more attracted (at least, in his middle years) to classical Greece than to Christianity. He speaks as often of 'the gods' as of God. Even in this interview, he is not speaking of 'God'

but of 'a God', and that provokes the question, 'What God?'.
Still, it is even less likely that he means Zeus or even all the gods of
Greece. Perhaps he means simply a divine revelation or showing
of some sort, a new event (*Ereignis*) of Being. This puts in
question my tentative introduction of the word 'eschatological'.
Heidegger's idea of the retrieval of the past and his attraction to
Nietzsche's eternal recurrence theory may well mean that the
coming God is a new advent of a God who has already come but
been forgotten, even the God of Christianity. Or the talk of a
coming God might be only Heidegger's way of suggesting a new
kairos of thinking, a new beginning for philosophy comparable
to its first beginning in Greece. But that would hardly be
confirmed by his apparent confession of the impotence of
philosophy to alter the state of the world, as expressed in the
quotations above. How far we have moved from the Promethean
utterances of Division Two of *Being and Time*!

But let us return to the conversation.

Heidegger: 'I see the essence of technology in what I call the
'framework', (*Ge-stell*), an expression which may be unfortun-
ate and is often ridiculed. The power of the framework means
that the human being is framed in, claimed and challenged by a
power which is revealed in the essence of technology and of
which he is not himself the master. To attain to this insight,
thinking is no longer required. Philosophy is at an end.'

Journalist: In earlier times – and not only in earlier times –
it was, after all, thought that philosophy could bring about
many things indirectly though only rarely directly, and that it
could help forward new movements to a breakthrough. If one
thinks only of the Germans, of the great names of Kant and
from Hegel to Nietzsche, to say nothing of Marx, then it can be
demonstrated that indirectly philosophy has had an immense
effect. Do you mean to say that now this efficacy of philosophy
is at an end? And if you say, the old philosophy is dead and is
no longer there, does this imply the thought that the efficacy of
philosophy, if ever there was such a thing, is there no longer
today?'

Heidegger: A mediate effect is possible through another

thinking, so that thinking alters the state of the world caus-
ally, as it were.

When I paused earlier to comment on the conversation between Heidegger and the journalists, I observed with some
satisfaction that the philosopher had departed far from the
Promethean attitudes that appeared in *Being and Time*, and
other writings of that period. Now, pausing again after quoting
some further paragraphs of the conversation, would it be
perverse of me to complain that Heidegger has reacted too
violently against the Promethean image? Christian theology
would agree that human effort and human ideology (including
the 'thinking' of philosophers) cannot of themselves save
mankind, but Heidegger seems to go far beyond this in the later
stages of his thinking. Responsibility is thrown back on a fate or
destiny, which remains obscure even if it is called by such names
as 'God' or 'Being' or 'Appropriation'. To quote one of
Heidegger's austere utterances: 'Whether God lives or remains
dead is not determined by the religiousness of man, and still less
by the theological aspirations of philosophy and science.
Whether God is God is determined from and within the constel-
lation of Being.'[29] God may withdraw as well as presence.

Pushed to extremes, this view becomes a fatalism, so that we
can only fold our hands and wait. But Heidegger does not quite
push it to extremes. There are two points at which 'another
thinking' might be invoked. One is his acknowledgment that, at
least, human beings can prepare themselves, can make themselves ready and open, for a new advent, a return of the divine.
God or Being or whatever name we use is not just a tyrannous
destiny but One who has called humanity into the light of truth
to be the shepherd who cares for the world, so that God and the
human race must work together, sharing the risks and the
possibilities of a world. The other point is that God and the
human being, or, if you prefer, *Sein* and *Dasein*, are both
temporal, not in the sense that beyond them both is a more
ultimate reality, time, but in the sense that both generate time
because they need time to project a future that will continue to
expand.

It would be wrong to claim that Heidegger's philosophy is a Christian philosophy – perhaps there is no such thing as a Christian philosophy. But it can be interpreted in a way that is compatible with Christian faith, and it can yield important insights into the faith.

Even when Heidegger speaks of 'the gods', may we not understand beyond the gods the ultimate God, just as Tillich and other Christian theologians have talked of the God who is beyond all our representations of Deity? Heidegger himself writes that 'the gods are the beckoning messengers of the Godhead', in himself incomparable and ineffable.[30]

A story that sometimes comes into my mind as I think of these things is that story in the Gospels of Christ walking on the water (Mark 6, 47–51; and parallels). Whatever incident may lie behind the story, it is above all a wonderful parable of the lives of human beings, thrown into a world in which they must live precariously with no ground of metaphysical certainty below their feet. And it is Christ who is walking on the sea – Christ who in the faith of the church is 'God with us', so that God too is walking on the sea. This is how we must see things if God, like ourselves, has his being in time. Bishop John Taylor comments on the story in these words: 'Insecurity is the place where God's presence becomes convincing reality, not because God looks for our abject dependence but simply because insecurity is the condition in which *God has placed himself*. A God who relies on the risks of potentiality for making and sustaining the universe and who copes with every reverse and disappointment with an unwearying *ad hoc* "Where shall we go from here?" is not a God of all certainty but a God of all hope.'[31]

8

Some Loose Ends

In this chapter I shall consider three matters which could not easily be incorporated into the main part of the book, yet they are at the same time questions which cannot be ignored. They are: the difficulties of translating Heidegger, because of the close connection between his thought and the German language; the involvement of Heidegger with National Socialism and how this might affect our judgment of his thought; and the relation of Heidegger to mysticism.

1. On translating Heidegger

It was almost an accident that led me into the labour of translating *Being and Time*. After serving in the British Army, I was inducted in 1948 to a small parish in the city of Brechin, situated in the north-east of Scotland. There, on the suggestion of one of my former professors, I began to work on a doctoral thesis on Rudolf Bultmann, probably the greatest New Testament scholar of the twentieth century. Bultmann was at that time still in the midst of writing his *Theology of the New Testament*. The supervisor of my researches, Professor Ian Henderson, advised me that if I wanted to understand Bultmann, I must first come to terms with the philosophy of Martin Heidegger, since Bultmann depended heavily upon him for his hermeneutic method. So I began reading *Sein und Zeit*, and found it both difficult and fascinating. Although I had a first-class honours degree in Mental Philosophy, I had never come across anything quite like this! As I worked through the book, I made a fairly detailed *précis* of its contents. I found that each chapter became more easily intelligible when one had read the chapter that followed. Of course, I then had to ask myself, 'What happens when one gets to the last chapter?'

When I had finished my dissertation and was arranging for publication, my publisher suggested that my next task might be to make, on the basis of my *précis*, a complete translation. I agreed to do so, though I must confess that it was not long before I began to doubt the wisdom of embarking on this undertaking. The next step came when my publisher discovered that an American philosopher, Edward S. Robinson, a professor at the University of Kansas, had also begun to work on a translation, and the question was raised whether we might co-operate in the work. We both thought that by working together, we might lighten the load and perhaps complete the translation more quickly. So although Robinson and I had not met at that time, we made what might be termed a 'blind date', and it turned out wonderfully well, for we became good friends and remained so until my collaborator was killed in a traffic accident in 1968. We were wrong, however, in thinking that collaboration would speed up the work. We spent much time in consultation about the translation of key-terms and of knotty passages, and the process of translation went on for seven years. If Robinson had lived, we would probably have undertaken a full revision, but I never felt that I wanted to do this on my own.

When we started out, we were given the impression by the German publishers that Heidegger did not care much whether his *magnum opus* got translated into English or not. He did sometimes express the opinion that only German and Greek are languages fit for serious philosophical discourse. Certainly some of the subtleties of his book defy translation into English, for they rely on peculiarities of German, especially etymologies. We have seen[1] that Heidegger regarded language as the 'house of Being', and reached some of his substantive philosophical conclusions from philological points. Let me give an example. He claims that *Sorge*, 'care', is a comprehensive concept for the being of *Dasein*. The same root appears in the words *Besorgen* and *Fürsorge*, denoting the special modes of care when it is directed to things and persons respectively, and rendered in the English translation by the words 'concern' and 'solicitude'. But these English renderings completely miss what leaps out at the reader of the German text – the fact that we are confronted with different manifestations of care.

As time went on, we gathered that Heidegger was becoming more interested in the translation. When the English version at last appeared in 1962, he sent to the publishers the following gracious letter (now in the possession of the present writer):

> Freiburg i.Br.-Zahringen,
> Rotebuck 47
> 28 Jan. 1965

S CM Press Ltd, Publishers,
  Direktor: David L. Edwards,
Bedford Square
London W Cı

Nachdem die von Ihnen veranlasste Übersetzung meiner Hauptschrift 'Sein und Zeit' sich jetzt in den english sprechenden Ländern verbreitet hat, möchte ich Ihnen meinen besonderen Dank übermitteln, dass Sie sich dieser Mühe unterzogen. Ganz besonders bitte ich darum, den beiden Herren, die die Übersetzung in einer langwierigen Arbeit ausführten, meinen Dank zu übermitteln. Wenn ich das jetzt erst tue, so bitte ich es damit zu entschuldigen, dass mir sehr viel daran lag, kompetente Urteile über die Übersetzung zu hören. Sie sind inzwischen von verschiedenen Seiten eingegangen. Ich weiss, wie schwer es ist, meine Arbeiten in einer anderen Sprache vorzulegen; ich bin darum besonders erfreut, das die Übersetzung so gut ausgeführt wurde. Der Absatz zeigt, eine wie grosse Lücke auf dem internationalen Büchermarkt wissenschaftlicher Werke mit dieser Übersetzung geschafften wurde.

Mit dem Wunsche erfolgreicher weiterer Arbeit.

> begrüsse ich Sie freundlich.

> Martin Heidegger

[Now that the translation which you arranged of my principal work *Being and Time* has become known in the English-speaking countries, I would like to convey to you my particular thanks for the trouble you have taken in undertaking this. I beg you especially to pass on my thanks to the two gentlemen who carried out the protracted labour of making the translation. If I am only now doing this, I beg you to excuse me, because it was important for me to hear competent judgments of the translation. These have now been received from various quarters. I know how difficult it is to present my works in another language; I am therefore especially pleased that the translation has been carried out so well. The sales show how great a need there is in the international book market for translations of academic works.

With cordial greetings and good wishes for future work,

Martin Heidegger]

2. *Heidegger and National Socialism*

As was mentioned in chapter 1,[2] Heidegger served for one year as Rector of Freiburg University after Hitler came to power in Germany in 1933. I promised that this episode would be more fully examined later in the book, and the point has now been reached when the promise must be fulfilled. I do not think that Heidegger's conduct at that time can be excused or glossed over but it is also important that we see this episode of his career in its correct proportions. I believe also that from my personal experience I can cite at least two points that will help us to achieve a fair view of the matter.

The facts are well enough known. Hitler and the National Socialists came to power by legitimate constitutional means early in 1933. In April Heidegger was appointed the Rector of Freiburg University, succeeding a rector who had been opposed to the Nazis. In May Heidegger joined the Party, though his appointment as rector indicates that he was already a supporter. We have a record of his public utterances during the time of his rectorship, and while they certainly express support for the regime, they are not extreme or fanatical and – very importantly – they do not contain any anti-Semitic utterances. I shall quote some of this material later.

In 1934, within a year of his appointment, Heidegger gave up the rectorship. His defenders claim that he left the party at this time. This is uncertain, but if he did, that was quite a significant act, as leaving the party at that time was to court the hostility of the authorities. His detractors claim that he continued his party membership until the end of World War II, but this is also uncertain. Because of his association with the Party during his rectorship, the occupying powers suspended him from university teaching in 1945. Five years later, however, he was restored, since it was decided that his involvement had not been of a serious active kind. That might well have been the end of the matter, but from time to time new accusations have been made, though in fact no convincing new evidence has been produced, one way or the other. The lapse of 1933 has remained as a question mark against Heidegger – it has been appropriately called by Michael Zimmermann 'the thorn in Heidegger's side'.[3] How important is it for our own inquiry? There are quite a few questions that have to be considered.

There is the general question of how far a person's teaching or the value of that teaching is affected by that person's conduct, or views held either privately or publicly. In many cases, there is conflict, and I find it hard myself to believe that a person can so compartmentalize his or her life that different areas of that life do not affect one another. Can, for instance, a politician who is unfaithful to his wife be entrusted with matters of state? Many people seem to be untroubled by such a situation, but this may simply reflect the lax morality of our times. But where the person concerned is teaching, let us say, ethics or theology, must we not expect that personal conduct and personal convictions should measure up to what that person teaches? Tillich is generally believed to have been something of a womanizer, and this would seem to argue that he lacked a proper respect for human personality; does this affect the value of his theology? Frege held extremely nationalistic and aggressive views, but does this matter when we evaluate his logic? Bloch's philosophy of hope has been utilized by Moltmann and by 'liberation' theologians, but he had an unreserved enthusiasm for the Stalinist dictatorship. Can these things be reconciled? The questions are not easy to answer. Both sides have been ably argued.

The reader will remember that I mentioned a conference held at Drew University in 1964 when the purpose was to discuss the relevance of Heidegger's philosophy of language for theological hermeneutics.[4] Heidegger himself had been billed to address the conference, but for medical reasons was unable to travel, and the limelight was taken by the eminent scholar Hans Jonas, a former student of Bultmann. *The New York Times* of 11 April had a sensational headline: 'Scholar breaks with Heidegger: Pro-Nazism is Charged'. In an impassioned address, Jonas claimed that Heidegger's associations with National Socialism had disqualified him for having anything relevant to say to theologians. Jonas' accusation was twofold: Heidegger, he claimed, was a fatalist for whom history is decreed by the force of destiny (*Geschick*); and God has been reduced to 'world' and is conceived as wholly immanent. I did myself[5] enter a *caveat* about Heidegger's introduction of the category of destiny when we first met it, though we have seen that he tries to combine it with an acknowledgment of human responsibility.[6] If a hidden destiny were the sole force shaping history, then this would, I think, be incompatible with Christianity. But one has to inquire how destiny and human decision are related in the historical process. Perhaps Heidegger's problem here is not very different from that of the Christian theologian who claims that the texture of events comes about by human decision working under an overruling divine providence. As for the view that in Heidegger God is entirely immanent (I suppose that would mean a form of pantheism), I do not think this is true. God (or whatever reality takes the place of God in Heidegger's thought) is indeed immanent in the beings and is nothing apart from the beings, but must not God be ontologically different from the beings? A spirited reply to Jonas was made by William J. Richardson in an article 'Heidegger and God – and Professor Jonas'.[7] I do not judge whether Richardson refuted Jonas in their exchange. But he asked: 'Why are Christians interested in Heidegger's thought?' He replied to his own question: 'Because there is truth in Heidegger and wherever there is truth, there is God ... What precisely that truth in Heidegger may be, may be difficult to say. Perhaps it is only a philosophical truth: the ontological difference as such. But that much would be gain. Perhaps there is in him a theological truth.'

Is there anything in Heidegger's thought that would justify the charges of Hans Jonas? If there is, then I think the weight of the charge rests in his first point, that Heidegger's view of history introduces a notion of destiny that becomes almost a rival God. Perhaps Heidegger thought that the 1930s were a *kairos*, a time of destiny for Germany. Perhaps he even came close to believing that he himself was destined to be the prophet and seer of the new age. But that is speculation, and from 1934 onward he became increasingly disillusioned with National Socialism. In his *Introduction to Metaphysics* (lectures given in 1935, published in 1953), occurs a passage which has occasioned much controversy. It reads: 'The works that are being peddled about nowadays as the philosophy of National Socialism but have nothing whatever to do with the inner truth and greatness of this movement (namely, the encounter between global technology and modern man) have all been written by men fishing in the troubled waters of "values" and "totalities".'[8] Do these words praise National Socialism, or do they condemn it for missing out on the truly great issue with which it should have been involved along with the whole human race, namely, 'the encounter between global technology and modern man'? There is an ambiguity here and it has not been resolved by desultory debate during five or six decades. Even if we go back to the speech which Heidegger gave at his inauguration as Rector of Freiburg University when his connection with the Party was at its closest, there is ambiguity. The speech bears the title, 'The Self-Assertion of the German Universities'.[9] The speech was a recall to the tradition of the German universities in the dangerous years preceding the War of 1939–45. Perhaps its climax was the following paragraph: 'In the future will flourish the threefold commitment and service of the German student body: first, in the community of the people through the Labour Service; second, to the honour of the nation through Army Service; and third in commitment to the spiritual order of the German people through the service of learning.' One may certainly say, 'This is nationalistic', but this kind of rhetoric was by no means peculiar to Heidegger in the threatening year of 1933. At least he does seem to sketch out a role for the universities that is wider than merely slavish obedience to the party-line.

I promised to bring to this discussion two items from my own experience, as these seem to throw some further light on Heidegger's situation.

In the three years immediately after the cessation of hostilities in 1945, the British Army authorities appointed me, because of my knowledge of the German language, to have oversight of chaplaincy services in the Prisoner of War camps in the Middle East. There were about 100,000 prisoners including some thirty chaplains who had served in various capacities in the German army. I spent a lot of time with these German prisoners, both the clerics and the lay people, and, among other things, gave lectures and answered the questions they asked. Very few among them, as far as I could discover, were hardened Nazis. Most of them had been pursuing peaceful and useful lives in Germany. But they had been caught up in the torrent of world events, which must have seemed to them like an irresistible destiny. Their country was in a desperate condition, and had been so since the end of World War I. They believed (perhaps rightly) that there was the serious danger of a communist take-over. It was fertile ground for Hitler's rhetoric, and, of course, in the early stages, the full enormities of his policies were not yet understood. I could not help coming to the conclusion that most of these men had simply drifted along with the Party. After all, the Germans had much less experience of democratic responsibility than had the British and the Americans.

The second point I want to make concerns a conversation I had with Dr Hannah Arendt, the distinguished political philosopher, who had been one of Heidegger's ablest students. I got to know her while engaged in the translation of *Being and Time*. Since Heidegger himself did not know English well, he suggested to Robinson and myself that if we had any special difficulties, we might contact Dr Arendt for help. She and I continued to have contacts after the translation was completed. Our last meeting took place on 19 May 1973. Dr Arendt was on her way to Europe for the summer vacation, and we agreed to meet at

Heathrow Airport, where she had to change planes. Our conversation turned naturally to Heidegger and to the translation. There had been surprisingly large sales and several reprintings in the United States, and I said to her, 'Heidegger must be making a lot of money from the translation.' She replied, 'Oh no. He's not a business man, and most of the money goes to the publisher.' I took her up on this: 'Would you say then that it was because he is not a man of affairs that he became involved with the Nazis in 1933?' 'Yes,' she said, 'quite so.'

Of course, it could be said that a man of his superior intelligence ought to have known better than to get involved with anything so disreputable and intellectually vacuous as National Socialism. That does not mean that he should have become a hero of the resistance or anything of that sort. Only a few have that kind of courage. But at the very least he should have followed the example of many other academics who remained silent and kept their integrity until better times should come. But the story now belongs to the past and should be laid to rest. Unfortunately we live in a time when mediocre journalists and frustrated academics take a perverse delight in debunking the great figures of the past. Even in the last two or three years they have dug up scandal or worse about Christopher Columbus, William Shakespeare, Albert Einstein, Martin Luther King. No one is free of faults and weaknesses, but we remember these men for their achievements, and these continue to stand. The same is true in Heidegger's case, and he is to be judged primarily by his thinking and the results which are still flowing from it.

3. Heidegger and mysticism

It is a more agreeable task to turn to the question of Heidegger's relation to mysticism, though once again there is a considerable measure of ambiguity. Mysticism itself is a very diversified phenomenon, though there are some characteristics that recur in the mysticisms associated with different religions. In Plotinus, one of the greatest mystics of the Western world and the inspiration behind that whole succession of mystics belonging to the neo-Platonist tradition, we find something very close to the 'ontological difference' between Being and the beings, a conception that is quite central to Heidegger. Thus we read in Plotinus: 'That which stands as primal source of everything is not a thing but is distinct from all things; it is not then a member of the total, but earlier than all, earlier even than intellect.'[10]

One might therefore claim that Heidegger and Plotinus (taken here as a representative mystic) have in view a similar ontological structure. This structure is twofold, on the one side Being or the One, not itself a being; on the other side, the multitude of finite beings that make up the world, among which dwells the human being or *Dasein* as not just another being but as that finite being which has some mysterious affinity to the Source – as Plotinus would put it, 'The intellect in us must rise to its origins',[11] or as Heidegger might put it, adapting Parmenides, 'Being and the thinking of Being are the same.'[12] In Heidegger's case, this 'thinking' is, in its meditative or contemplative character, something like the mental prayer of the mystic as we noted in connection with his own phrase, 'the piety of thinking'.[13]

Of course, one must not press these similarities too far. Heidegger continued to view himself as a thinker, and perhaps the thinker must retain a certain space between himself and what is thought, or, in other words, perhaps he has not quite got away from objectification, even from metaphysics, to mention Heidegger's particular fear. The true mystic seems to throw himself or herself into the Absolute with an abandon which has left even the highest levels of thought behind. According to Plotinus, 'Only by a leap can we reach to the One.'[14] Is there anything corresponding to this in Heidegger? The nearest that he comes to it is in his lecture 'What is Metaphysics?' with its postscript. There he faces the question whether he has abandoned logic. His answer is that 'logic is only *one* exposition of the nature of thinking . . . The idea of logic gets dissolved in the vortex of a more primordial inquiry.'[15] There is another and, in his view, more profound thinking that is responsive, and, as we have seen, close to thanking. So although he continued to regard himself as a thinker, his 'thought' was not ordinary logical thought nor yet was it a mystical immersion in the Absolute.

An excellent study of what may be called Heidegger's spirituality has been provided by Michael Zimmerman. The book is called *Eclipse of the Self*, and this title indicates a process in which egocentricity is gradually overcome. Zimmermann holds that 'inauthenticity is an intensification of everyday egosim; authenticity is a diminution of it'.[16] The progression is from the understanding of the self as something solid and closed to the understanding of the self as finite openness. In this openness, there is a relation to Being comparable to the mystic's relation to God. This comparison has been contested on the ground that in Heidegger there seems to be no personal or loving element in the relation of the *Dasein* to Being or the Event or however one designates the Ultimate Reality in Heidegger's philosophy. But Zimmermann points out that 'Heidegger's releasement is a gift or loving bestowal which allows us to think, thank and love. He refused to personalize the Event (*Ereignis*) because this would have the effect of treating it as a being. Even for Eckhart, the Godhead lacks the personal character we attribute to God as Father, Son and Holy Spirit, for the three persons are merged in the one undifferentiated essence.'[17]

Zimmermann's mention of Eckhart raises the question of Heidegger's relation to mediaeval Christian mysticism. Heidegger mentioned Eckhart in several of his writings and both men, I believe, show the influence of the neo-Platonist tradition. The most thorough exploration of Heidegger's relation to mediaeval mysticism that I know is the dissertation of Dr Sonya Sitta, entitled *Three Forms of Transcendence: A Study of Heidegger and Medieval Theology*. In this work the author shows in masterly fashion both the similarities and the differences between Heidegger and the mystics.[18]

Writers on mysticism have been in broad agreement that one of its distinguishing marks is a vision of the unity of all things. For instance, W. T. Stace declares, 'The sense of unity is a nuclear and essential characteristic of mystical experiences',[19] while H. A. Hodges says, 'The mystic is one who sees the deep-seated unity which things have by their common derivation from and utter dependence on the Ultimate, and who wishes to be drawn experientially nearer to the centre of that unity than he is now.'[20]

One could hardly say, however, that the notion of the unity of all things is central in Heidegger's thought. Rather, the experience of beings in their totality comes in the mood of anxiety or dread (*Angst*) and is one aspect of the experience of the nothing. We again refer to the lecture, 'What is Metaphysics?' where we read: 'In anxiety, as we say, "one feels something uncanny." We are unable to say what gives one that uncanny feeling. One just feels it generally (*im Ganzen*). All things, and we with them, sink into a kind of indifference. But not in the sense that everything disappears; rather, in the very act of drawing away from us everything turns toward us. The withdrawal of beings in their totality, which then crowd round us in our anxiety, this is what oppresses us. There is nothing to hold on to. The only thing that remains and overwhelms us while the beings slip away, is this "nothing". Anxiety reveals nothing.'[21] This nothing, of course, is Being, which is indeed no thing. It is also called the 'veil' of Being.

These sentences remind us of Heidegger's conversation with a Japanese scholar who said to him, 'For us, the void is the highest name for what you call Being.'[22] Is Heidegger then closer to Eastern than to Western mysticism? Certainly his works have been widely studied in Japan and other Eastern countries. Yet in spite of the obvious affinity that some Eastern scholars feel for Heidegger, there are clearly differences here also, just as we found them in his relation to Western mystics. Keiji Nishitani, a leading representative of the Kyoto school of philosophy (he may possibly have been Heidegger's interlocutor in the dialogue quoted above, for he spent three years studying with Heidegger) writes: 'In Heidegger's case, traces of the representation of nothingness as some "thing" that is nothingness still remain.'[23] I feel sure Heidegger would resist this verdict. This thinker who made so much of truth as 'unconcealedness' leaves many of his own beliefs at least partially concealed. Perhaps it could not be otherwise, if one is to respect the mystery of Being. So to the question, 'Was Heidegger a mystic?' we can only reply that he had some affinities to the mystics. He comes closest to them when he translates that cryptic saying of Parmenides as, 'Being and the thinking of Being are the same',[24] and when, in another place, he adds the clarification that 'Being is not a product of thinking; it is more likely that essential thinking is an event (*Ereignis*) of Being.'[25]

Notes

1. Career and Early Writings

1. G. S. Kirk and J. E. Raven, *The Presocratic Philosophers: A Critical History with a Selection of Texts*, Cambridge University Press 1960, p. 197.
2. Ibid., p. 191.
3. This anecdote is preserved by Aristotle, *Basic Works*, ed. Richard McKeon, Random House, New York 1941, p. 657. It is quoted by Heidegger in *LH*.
4. Kirk and Raven, p. 279.
5. Ibid., p. 269.
6. *HCT*, p. 236.
7. *BT*, p. 171.
8. *CL*, p. 71.
9. *US*, p. 96.
10. *TB*, p. 74.
11. Ibid., pp. 79–80.
12. See Charles Guignon (ed.), *The Cambridge Companion to Heidegger*, Cambridge University Press 1993, p. 287, n. 15.
13. Hans-Georg Gadamer, 'Anrufung des entschwundenen Gottes,' in *Evangelische Kommentare*, vol. 10 (1977), pp. 204–8.
14. K. Löwith, *From Hegel to Nietzsche*, tr. D. E. Green, Doubleday, Garden City 1967, p. 207.
15. *HCT*, p. 136.
16. Ibid., p. 307.
17. Richard Kroner, 'Heidegger's Private Religion' in *Union Seminary Quarterly Review*, vol. 11, no. 4 (1956), p. 24.
18. *BT*, p. 488.
19. In Guignon, p. 272.
20. See n. 17, above.
21. Quotations are from the English translation by Michael Heron in *Envoy*, vol. 3, no. 11 (1950), pp. 71–5.

2. Being and Time (1)

1. 'The Essence of Truth,' in *EB*, ed. Werner Brock, Gateway Books, Chicago 1949, p. 316.
2. 'Existentialism is a Humanism' is the title of an essay by Sartre, in *Existentialism from Dostoyevsky to Sartre*, ed. and tr. W. Kaufmann, Meridian Books, Cleveland 1956, pp. 287–311.
3. *BT*, p. 19.
4. St Thomas Aquinas, *Summa Theologiae* 1a2ae, 94, 2.
5. *BT*, p. 67.
6. Ibid., pp. 74–5.
7. The subject of phenomenology would require a book in itself, and cannot be treated in any detail here. In spite of what has been said in chapter 1 about the ambiguity of Heidegger's remarks on phenomenology in *HCT*, there is a quite detailed account of how Heidegger understood the importance of phenomenology in that book, pp. 13–131.
8. *BT*, pp. 96–7.
9. Ibid., p. 170.
10. Ibid., p. 182.
11. Ibid., p. 272.
12. *HCT*, p. 60.
13. *BT*, p. 220.
14. Ibid., p. 68.
15. Ibid., p. 224.
16. Ibid., p. 225.
17. Ibid., p. 232.
18. Ibid., p. 237

3. Being and Time (2)

1. *BT*, p. 274.
2. Richard Kroner, 'Heidegger's Private Religion' in *Union Seminary Quarterly Review*, vol. 11, no. 4 (1956), p. 24.
3. *BT*, p. 292.
4. Ibid., p. 284.
5. Ibid., p. 310.
6. Ibid., p. 311.
7. Ibid., p. 303.
8. Ibid., p. 320.
9. Jean-Paul Sartre, *Being and Nothingness*, tr. Hazel E. Barnes, Philosophical Library, New York 1956, p. 615.
10. See above, p. 16.
11. *BT*, p. 358.

12. Frederick A. Olafson in Guignon, p. 103.
13. *BT*, p. 499.
14. Ibid., p. 432.
15. Martin Heidegger, *Nietzsche*. See Bibliography for particulars.
16. *BT*, p. 437.
17. See above, pp. 112–17.

4. *Metaphysics and Theology*

1. *WM*, p. 27. Of the three translations, the first is in *EB*, p. 329; the second in *BW*, p. 98; the third is my own suggested alternative.
2. *EB*, p. 330.
3. *EB*, p. 336, and *BW*, p. 103.
4. *BW*, p. 104.
5. Ibid., p. 105.
6. Ibid., p. 109.
7. Ibid., p. 112.
8. *EB*, p. 352.
9. Ibid., p. 353; *WM*, p. 45.
10. Ibid., pp. 336, 360.
11. Ibid., p. 335.
12. Ibid.
13. Ibid., p. 360.
14. Ibid., p. 359.
15. *WM*, p. 7.
16. *EB*, p. 354.
17. See 1949 edition of *WM*, p. 46. Cf. W. J. Richardson, *Heidegger: Through Phenomenology to Thought*, Martinus Nijhoff, The Hague 1963, pp. 562–5.
18. *IM*, p. 7.
19. The term is first used in *ID*, but the concept is already there in *IM*.
20. *ID*, p. 55.
21. In his memorial address. See above, chapter 1, n. 13.
22. *IM*, p. 155.
23. See above, pp. 2–3.
24. *IM*, p. 203.
25. *BW*, pp. 195–6.
26. Ibid., p. 196.
27. Ibid., pp. 196–7.
28. Ibid., p. 208.
29. *BT*, p. 255.
30. Quoted in *BW*, p. 213.
31. *BW*, p. 214.

32. Ibid., p. 221. In the German text of *LH*, this reads: 'Der Mensch ist nicht der Herr des Seienden. Der Mensch ist der Hirt des Seins.'
33. Ibid., pp. 233–4.

5. *Thinghood, Technology, Art*

1. See above, p. 21
2. *BT*, p. 95ff.
3. *BT*, pp. 96–7.
4. *BT*, p. 100.
5. 'Das Ding,' in *VA*, pp. 163–81.
6. See above, pp. 13–14.
7. *BW*, p. 221.
8. *VA*, pp. 170ff.
9. Aristotle, *Phys.* II, 3, in *Basic Works*, pp. 240–2.
10. See above, p. 53.
11. 'The Question concerning Technology,' in *BW*, pp. 283–317.
12. *BW*, pp. 297–8.
13. *BW*, pp. 300, 306.
14. *BW*, p. 306.
15. The full German text is in *HW*, pp. 7–68. English translation, slightly abridged, in *BW*, pp. 143–87.
16. *BW*, p. 185.
17. Ibid., p. 149.
18. See above, pp. 65–7.
19. *BW*, p, 163.
20. Ibid., pp. 164–5.
21. Ibid., p. 165.
22. Ibid., p. 168.
23. Ibid., p. 169.
24. Ibid., p. 170.

6. *Thinking, Language, Poetry*

1. *BT*, pp. 49–63.
2. W. J. Richardson, *Heidegger: from Phenomenology to Thought*, p. 47.
3. *WCT*, p. 8.
4. *EB*, p. 353.
5. See above, pp. 54–6.
6. See bibliography for particulars.
7. *WCT*, pp. 113–14.
8. Ibid., p. 3.

9. In *TB*, pp. 55–73.

10. See above, p. 3.

11. *WCT*, pp. 14–17, 23.

12. Ibid., pp. 79–80.

13. Ibid., p. 141.

14. *The Piety of Thinking* is the title given to a collection of Heidegger's writings on theology. See bibliography.

15. See bibliography for particulars.

16. *DT*, p. 46. Cf. what is said here with the remarks on technology and the River Rhine, p. 69 above.

17. See above, pp. 36–8.

18. *DT*, pp. 60–1.

19. Ibid., p. 81.

20. See above, p. 27.

21. *IM*, p. 156.

22. See above, p. 3.

23. *BW*, p. 199.

24. *US*, p. 241.

25. *BT*, p. 47.

26. *US*, p. 166.

27. *BT*, pp. 27–8.

28. Ibid., pp. 55–8.

29. *IM*, pp. 124–5.

30. *WCT*, pp. 198ff.

31. See above, p. 18.

32. *US*, p. 96.

33. Ibid., p. 109.

34. See above, p. 71.

35. J. G. Hamann, *Aesthetica in Nuce*, in R. G. Smith, ed., *J. G. Hamann: A Study in Christian Existence, with Selections from his Writings*, p. 196.

36. See above, p. 45.

37. *EB*, p. 284.

38. For the English-speaking reader, Hölderlin's work is most easily accessible in his *Selected Verse*, ed. Michael Hamburger, Penguin Books 1961. This edition gives German texts with English translations. About ten of Hölderlin's poems are included in *The Oxford Book of German Verse*, ed. E. L. Stahl, Oxford University Press 1967³. Although I have confined this discussion of Heidegger's appreciation for poetry to his reactions to Hölderlin, other poets too made a strong impression, notably Stefan George (1868–1933) and Georg Trakl (1887–1914).

39. *EH*, p. 95.

40. See above, p. 61.

7. 'Only a God Can Save Us'

1. See above, p. 60.
2. R. Kearney and J. S. O'Leary (eds), *Heidegger et la Question de Dieu*, Grasset 1980.
3. See my *In Search of Deity*, SCM Press and Crossroad 1984, pp. 163ff.
4. See above, pp. 14–15.
5. See above, p. 5.
6. See above, p. 7.
7. The English-language volume, *On Time and Being*, tr. Joan Stambaugh, Harper & Row 1972 contains the essays, 'Time and Being' and 'The End of Philosophy'.
8. *EB*, p. 353.
9. *TB*, p. 2.
10. Ibid., p. 3.
11. See above, pp. 59–60.
12. *TB*, p. 5.
13. *In Search of Deity*, pp. 153ff.
14. John Scotus Eruigena, *Periphyseon*, ed. I. P. Sheldon-Williams, Dublin Institute for Advanced Studies 1968, 426 C–D.
15. See above, p. 60.
16. John R. Williams, *Martin Heidegger's Philosophy of Religion*, Wilfrid Laurier University Press 1977, p. 154.
17. *TB*, p. 8.
18. Ibid., p. 19.
19. Ibid., p. 22.
20. The paper is included in the collection, *The Piety of Thinking*, ed. J. G. Hart and J. C. Maraldo, Indiana University Press 1976. Abbreviated in references as *PT*.
21. *PT*, p. 22.
22. Ibid.
23. Ibid., p. 23.
24. Ibid., p. 24.
25. Ibid., p. 26.
26. Ibid., p. 27.
27. Ibid.
28. 'Nur noch ein Gott kann uns retten: Spiegel-Gespräch mit Martin Heidegger am 23. September, 1966.' Published in *Der Spiegel*, no. 26, 31 May 1976, pp. 193–219.
29. *Die Technik und die Kehre*, Neske 1962, p. 46.
30. *VA*, p. 177.
31. John V. Taylor, *The Christlike God*, SCM Press 1992, p. 194.

8. *Some Loose Ends*

1. See above, pp. 85ff.
2. See above, p. 10.
3. Michael Zimmermann, 'The Thorn in Heidegger's Side: The Question of National Socialism,' in *Philosophical Forum*, vol. 20 (1989), pp. 326–65.
4. See above, pp. 101–4.
5. See above, pp. 45–6.
6. See above, p. 69.
7. W. J. Richardson, 'Heidegger and God – and Professor Jonas,' in *Thought*, vol. 40 (1965), pp. 13–40.
8. *IM*, p. 199.
9. In *GE*, pp. 18–20.
10. Plotinus, *Enneads* V, 3, 11.
11. Ibid., III, 8, 9.
12. See above, p. 3.
13. See above, p. 82.
14. Plotinus, *Enneads* V, 5, 5.
15. *EB*, pp. 342, 356.
16. M. Zimmermann, *Eclipse of the Self*, Ohio University Press 1981, p. 47.
17. Ibid., pp. 248–9.
18. Dr Sitta's dissertation (not yet published) was submitted to the University of York.
19. W. T. Stace, *Mysticism and Philosophy*, Macmillan 1960, p. 83.
20. H. A. Hodges, *God beyond Knowledge*, Macmillan 1979, p. 106.
21. *EB*, p. 336.
22. See above, pp. 88–9.
23. Keiji Nishitani, *Religion and Nothingness*, tr. Jan van Bragt, University of California Press 1982, p. 96.
24. See above, p. 3.
25. *EB*, p. 356. For the meaning of *Ereignis*, see above, pp. 100–1.

Bibliography

1. Writings of Martin Heidegger

This bibliography contains only works cited in the text. These works are indicated in the notes by abbreviations, e.g., *Being and Time* appears as *BT*. Citations are usually from the English translations, where available, but in some cases I have made my own translations from the German texts. In the list which follows, the identifying abbreviation appears, then the full title and details of publication. The complete edition of Heidegger's work is still in progress of publication. At the end of each item, the letters GA (Gesamtausgabe) followed by a number indicates the volume containing that item in the complete edition. About 100 volumes are planned, the publisher is Vittorio Klostermann, Frankfurt-am-Main, and the information given here was correct at the end of 1992.

BP   *Die Grundprobleme der Phanomenologie*, Vittorio Klostermann, 1975 (Lectures given in 1927).
      English: *Basic Problems of Phenomenology*, tr. A. Hofstadter, Indiana University Press, Bloomington 1982.

GA24 (1989)

BT   *Sein und Zeit*, Max Niemeyer, Tubingen 1927.
      English: *Being and Time*, SCM Press, London; Blackwell, Oxford; Harper & Row, New York 1962.

GA2 (1977)

BW   English only: *Basic Writings*, ed. D. F. Krell, various translators, Harper & Row; Routledge & Kegan Paul, London 1977. (Contains 'What is Metaphysics?' 'On the Essence of Truth,' 'The Origin of the Work of Art,' 'Letter on Humanism,' 'The Question concerning Technology,' etc.)

CL   *Der Feldweg*, Klostermann 1953, (written about 1949 and first circulated privately).

English: 'The Country Lane', tr. Michael Heron, in *Envoy*, vol. 3, no. 11, pp. 71–5.

DT   *Gelassenheit*, Günther Neske, Pfullingen 1959.
English: *Discourse on Thinking*, tr. J. M. Anderson and E. H. Freund. Harper & Row 1966.

EB   English only: *Existence and Being*, ed. Werner Brock, various translators. Henry Regnery, Chicago 1949. (Contains 'On the Essence of Truth,' 'Remembrance of the Poet,' 'Hölderlin and the Essence of Poetry,' 'What is Metaphysics?' with postscript.)

EH   *Erläuterungen zu Hölderlins Dichtung*, Klostermann 1944.

FW   See *CL*.

GE   English only: *German Existentialism*, tr. D. D. Runes, Philosophical Library, New York 1965. (Contains 'The Self-Assertion of the German Universities' and other speeches relating to the Rectorate. The original German text of the rectoral address was published in 1933 by Korn, Breslau.)

HCT   *Prolegomena zur Geschichte des Zeitbegriffs*, (Lectures given in 1925).

GA20 (1988)
History of the Concept of Time, Indiana University Press 1992.

HW   *Holzwege*, Klostermann 1950. (Six long essays, including 'Der Ursprung des Kunstwerkes'. See *BW*.)

GA5 (1977)

ID   *Identität und Differenz*, Neske 1957
English: *Identity and Difference*, Harper & Row 1969.

GA11 (1978)

IM   *Einführung in die Metaphysik*, Niemeyer 1953 (Lectures given in 1935).
English: *Introduction to Metaphysics*, tr. Ralph Mannheim, Yale University Press 1959.

GA40 (1983)

KPM   *Kant und das Problem der Metaphysik*, Cohen, Bonn 1929.
English: *Kant and the Problem of Metaphysics*, tr. J. S. Churchill, Indiana University Press.

GA3 (1991)

LH   'Letter on Humanism' in *BW*. See *UH*, below.

N   *Nietzsche,*, 2 vols, Neske 1961
English: *Nietzsche*, 4 vols, tr. D. F. Krell, Harper & Row
1979–82.
                                             GA6, 43, 44

PT   English only: *The Piety of Thinking*, tr. J. G. Hart and
J. C. Maraldo, Indiana University Press 1976. (Essays on theology
written between 1929 and 1964.)

QCT   'The Question concerning Technology,' see *BW* and *VA*.

TB   *On Time and Being*, tr. Joan Stambaugh, Harper & Row 1972,
contains the essays 'Time and Being' and 'The End of philosophy
and the Task of Thinking.' See *VA*.

UH   *Über den Humanismus*, Klostermann 1947. See also *BW*.

US   *Unterwegs zur Sprache*, Neske 1954.
English: *On the Way to Language*, tr. P. D. Hertz, Harper & Row
1971.
                                            GA12 (1985)

VA   *Vorträge und Aufsätze*, Neske 1954. (An important collection of
essays. English versions of some of them in *BW* and *TB*.)
                                            GA7

WCT   *Was heisst Denken?* Niemeyer 1954.
English: *What Is Called Thinking?*, tr. F. D. Wieck and
J. G. Gray, Harper & Row 1954.
                                            GA8

WM   *Was Ist Metaphysik?*, Klostermann 1949. (Text of lecture given in
1929, with postscript added in 1943 and introduction added in
1949.)
English in *EB* (with postscript only) and in *BW* (with neither
postscript nor introduction).

WW   *Das Wesen der Wahrheit*, Klostermann 1930.
English: 'The Essence of Truth' in *EB* and *BW*.

2. Writings about Martin Heidegger

Biemel, Walter, *Martin Heidegger: An Illustrated Study*, tr. J. L. Mehta, Routledge 1977.

Caputo, John D, *Heidegger and Aquinas, An Essay on Overcoming Metaphysics*, Fordham University Press 1982.

Fell, Joseph P., *Heidegger and Sartre An Essay on Being and Place*, Columbia University Press 1979.

Gadamer, H. -G., 'Anrufung des entschwundenen Gottes,' in *Evangelische Kommentare*, vol. 10 (1977), pp. 204–8.

Gelven, Michael, *A Commentary on Heidegger's Being and Time*, Harper & Row 1970.

Grene, Marjorie, *Martin Heidegger*, Bowes & Bowes 1957.

Guignon, Charles (ed.), *The Cambridge Companion to Heidegger*, Cambridge University Press 1993.

Kearney, Richard and O'Leary, J. S. (ed.), *Heidegger et la Question de Dieu*, Grasset 1980.

Kroner, Richard, 'Heidegger's Private Religion,' in *Union Seminary Quarterly Review*, vol. 11 (1956), no. 4, p. 24.

Langan, Thomas, *The Meaning of Heidegger A Critical Study of an Existentialist Phenomenology*, Columbia University Press 1959.

Macquarrie, John, *An Existentialist Theology: A Comparison of Heidegger and Bultmann*, SCM Press 1955.

Macquarrie, John, *Martin Heidegger*, Lutterworth Press 1968.

Marx, Werner, *Heidegger und die Tradition*, Niemeyer 1962.

Ott, Hugo, *Heidegger: A Political Life*, tr. Allan Blunden, HarperCollins 1993.

Richardson, W. J., *Heidegger: Through Phenomenology to Thought*, Nijhoff 1963.

Seidel, George J., *Martin Heidegger and the Presocratics*, University of Nebraska Press 1964.

Versenyi, Laszlo, *Heidegger, Being and Truth*, Yale University Press 1965.

Vycinas, Vincent, *Earth and Gods: An Introduction to the Philosophy of Martin Heidegger*, Nijhoff 1961.

Waelhens, A. de, *La Philosophie de Martin Heidegger*, Publications Universitaires de Louvain 1942.

Zimmermann, Michael, *Eclipse of the Self*, Ohio University Press 1981.

Index